Creating Confidence
—— IN ——
WOMEN

Creating Confidence
—— IN ——
WOMEN

JENNIFER BERESFORD

First published in Great Britain 1998
SPCK
Holy Trinity Church
Marylebone Road
London NW1 4DU

The author and publisher would like to thank the following for permission
to use material in this book:
Arrow Books, *I'm OK, You're OK*, Thomas A. Harris, 1997.
Words from *The Prophet* by Kahlil Gibran are used by permission from
The National Committee of Gibran 1951, © all rights reserved.
Faber and Faber Ltd, 'Ash Wednesday', in *Collected Poems 1909–1962*,
T. S. Eliot, 1963.
Unpublished poem, 'My Dreams', Dorothy Tinsley, 1996.
Unpublished material from training courses run by Linda Richardson.

British Library Cataloguing in Publication Data

A catalogue record for this book is available from the British Library.

ISBN 0-281-05146-1

Typeset by Pioneer Associates, Perthshire
Printed in Great Britain by
The Cromwell Press, Melksham, Wiltshire

Contents

*For my daughter Emma, my step-daughter Charlotte
and my granddaughters
Rebecca, Katharine and Kate*

—— *Acknowledgements* ——

The Ecumenical Decade of Churches in Solidarity with Women 1988–1998 was intended to give the churches an opportunity to listen to women, to act upon what they said, and to enable them to use their gifts. It was also intended to empower women and to challenge discrimination in the churches and in society.

I have chaired the Oxford committee of this project for the last six years. As part of our programme we decided to set up 'confidence courses' for women. I am grateful to Rosemary Tucker for encouraging me to devise and run these courses with her, and to Linda Richardson for permission to use her material as a basis both for the courses and this book.

All the members of the committee have been supportive over the book, and my thanks to them all, especially Jo. Saunders, Rosemary Peirce and Susan Cole-King. Keith Lamden, Hilary Baker and Barbara Hayes have made valuable suggestions. Anne Borrowdale has been an excellent and generous reader for SPCK, and has contributed a great deal and been a real help to me.

My prayer group and other friends have contributed ideas and stories and Anne Bowker has given invaluable help with quotes.

My thanks too to Bishop Richard Harries for the foreword and to Monica Furlong for the introduction. I admire them both and am delighted that they agreed to help.

I became a practising Christian at Bishop Strachan School, Toronto, during the war. Since then I have been greatly helped on my journey by the community at Taizé, by David Barton, John Hadley, Philip Roderick, and the various clergy of the Hambleden Valley. I will always be grateful to them.

My family have been wonderfully supportive, Emma and Francis as critical but encouraging readers, and Simon as my patient computer tutor. My husband, Christopher, has given me every kind of loving, patient help, from grammar corrections to shopping and housekeeping. You have all been great. Thank you.

—— *Foreword* ——

It took some time for the idea of a decade of solidarity with women to catch on. One of the reasons we tried to think seriously about this in the diocese of Oxford was the initiative of Jennifer Beresford. Out of her experience has come this book, which many will find extremely helpful. It is readable, practical and directly addressed to the needs of so many. It is also firmly set within a Christian framework with some nice touches of humour. Reading it will literally be life-changing for a good many people.

Richard Harries, Bishop of Oxford

—— *Introduction* ——

The idea of assertiveness as a good thing has come late to women in history, and even later to women in the churches. As Jennifer Beresford points out, much mileage has been made in Christianity out of passivity and obedience as the desirable behaviour for women; Mary at the Annunciation, or waiting, traumatized, at Calvary, has been endlessly held up as the model. There has been strikingly less emphasis on energetic, purposeful models: Mary Magdalen announcing the Resurrection to the disciples, the logic-chopping Syro-Phoenician woman, or even the mother of Jesus herself, when her life is considered as a whole (there was certainly more to her than meekness, silence and suffering). In Christian history the quiet, selfless woman who always did what she was told, and was always 'serving', won out over any other possibility of 'being' for women who wanted social approval (which, of course, all human beings do). Lively, articulate, creative women who did not fit into this model of modest womanhood suffered a good deal in trying to force themselves into an improbable mould.

What the churches are painfully recognizing in these last years of the twentieth century is the way, sometimes consciously, but mainly unconsciously, we have used religion as a form of control – of women, 'the lower classes', 'natives' in our former colonies, and of sexuality in general. We now see that Christians have behaved coercively, manipulatively, and more out of fear than love, and we have a lot of difficult rethinking and reliving to do. Because none of us are innocent of having victimized others or letting ourselves become victims, this is embarrassing and painful. Yet, as we begin to make changes, our work becomes profoundly rewarding in setting us and others free.

I believe that Jennifer Beresford's book will play a very useful part in this fundamental change. I like the essential simplicity of her argument, that in the old days, and indeed up to the present time, women paid too high a price for their complicity in an all-male authority – in frustration, depression, wasted talent, loss of self-esteem and bitter resentment. (Men, of course, have suffered too, since an angry, miserable partner or mother is no pleasure to live with, particularly if she begrudges you a freer life.)

The book offers simple, practical steps, first in self-examination, then in moving towards greater self-assurance, born of under-standing. Jennifer has had a long experience of working with women. It has taught her that very few women, even 'achiev-ers', move comfortably and confidently through life. Most tend to suffer from guilt if they try to care for themselves, feel that they can never do enough to please others, often dislike their own bodies (which do not conform to some supposed male ideal), and, because of lack of confidence, are timid at attempt-ing new things. She decided that churches were good places to encourage women to greater assertiveness and personal fulfil-ment, and was delighted to discover that women often needed little more than interest and encouragement to move onto new achievements in work, family and social life.

Now the fruit of Jennifer's work in the Oxford diocese is available to us all in this succinct and valuable little book. I thoroughly enjoyed working through it, and noting the areas in which I could do with a bit more assertiveness – mainly in saying no, I discovered – and I feel that it should have a long and very useful future in church discussion groups, on book-stalls, and in the private reading of women and men who think that Christianity is about transformation of life, and not about keeping people in their place.

Monica Furlong

Chapter 1

Self-confidence in
—— Christian Women ——

I have come that you may have life, and have it in all
its fullness.

John 10.10

Why confidence?

In a small village hall 12 women meet every Tuesday for four
sessions. (The first evening, they arrive looking a bit appre-
hensive.) Sometimes they sit in a circle while the tutor explains
a new idea about 'ways that we behave'. There is discussion,
stories are told, an occasional tear is wiped away, but there is
much laughter and a great feeling of solidarity and mutual support. The women also share their experiences in small groups
of two or three. At one point they all stand up and say, loudly
and with increasing conviction, 'I am a strong, loving, gifted
woman and God loves me.' There are hand-outs to take home
and think about and questionnaires to fill in and keep privately.
Each session ends with 'the Grace', where they wish each
other the peace and love of God. They emerge chatting, relaxed
and looking a little taller.

This is a snapshot of one of the 'confidence courses' I have
helped run. When I met one of the group members in the high
street, several months later, she said, 'That course changed my
life!'

During the whole of my working life I was a social worker.

1

My title changed, but the job always involved working with families, especially mothers, most of whom had had few opportunities in the past and were now in some kind of distress. Almost always, a very low level of self-confidence added to their problems. Sometimes working to improve their self-esteem enabled them to overcome their difficulties by their own efforts. The support of other women in a group was often essential, and I led many different support groups.

> One day a woman came to a 'mothers' group' who was so depressed and miserable that she sat curled up, head down, on the verge of tears. She seemed frozen and unreachable in her misery. I asked each member of the group to say something they liked about her. As they did so she very gradually uncurled, raised her head, sat straighter and, eventually, smiled. It was as if the warmth of the others' kindness, concern and genuine affection had thawed her and given her a new sense of her own value.

This is a true story, as are others in this book. They come either from my own experience or that of friends. Only the names have been changed.

Although apparently confident in my work, I still suffer agonies of shyness in some social situations. My husband is now used to my pleas to go home when we arrive on our host's doorstep for a party – 'Perhaps it is the wrong night', 'Do we need to go?' It is the feeling of inadequacy: who will I talk to? Who will want to talk to me? I know how it feels and I don't like it!

Having run several confidence courses over the past few years, and encouraged by the enthusiastic response of many of the participants, I am determined to make these liberating skills more widely available. There are a number of these kind of courses, many coming from the United States, and some in women's magazines, but this book is about introducing confidence skills to Christian women.

The courses a colleague and I ran for church women were a

response to endless stories about men putting down, or patronizing, women who did not like to defend themselves for fear of seeming aggressive, feminist or unchristian. Women complain, but what do they do? Often they act passively, agreeing with or apologizing to the man, but grumbling to each other behind his back. Sadly, it is sometimes women who put other women down. Believing that we do not need to be martyrs, but need to be given the strength to deal directly with chauvinistic attitudes, my colleague and I devised and ran short, introductory sessions to raise self-esteem and teach assertiveness skills in a Christian framework.

It took some time to get these courses for women accepted by our local Christian training schemes, partly because the word 'assertive' sounds so like 'aggressive' that the two are often confused. *Aggressive* behaviour frightens both men and women. It involves standing up for our personal rights in a way which does not consider or respect the feelings of other people. *Assertive* behaviour, which this book teaches and advocates, involves recognizing your own needs, valuing them and meeting them as far as possible, bearing in mind the needs of others. It means empathizing with them – understanding with the heart, not just the head – and respecting them, loving your neighbour and yourself.

If we have confidence in ourselves, in our own vision, we can believe that God loves us in spite of our faults and short-comings, and we can work for the coming of his Kingdom. We can trust our insights and pursue our personal visions. How much self-esteem we have affects all aspects of our lives and all our relationships, even our relationship with God. Good self-esteem enables us to be loving, honest and generous and become more nearly the people we really want to be. It also enables us to make decisions.

Clearly, it is not just women who need self-esteem. Everyone does – men, women and children. Self-esteem allows individuals to learn more, achieve more, enjoy more, care more, relate better and generally live more responsible, happy and fulfilled lives. If we lack the basic confidence to recognize our personal worth, we are likely to be so defended and defensive, guarding our vulnerability behind a screen of indifference, or so frightened of being criticized that we cannot change or grow.

I believe that confidence skills should be taught in every school and the self-esteem of pupils actively nurtured (courses are available). This might reduce bullying and destructive behaviour and increase incentive to learn. There might also be fewer exclusions of disruptive children from schools. Our prisons and mental hospitals are filled not with people who feel they are liked, wanted and accepted, but with those who feel deeply inadequate, disliked, unwanted, unacceptable and unable.

Why especially for women?

All women benefit from improved self-esteem. For example, single women must face the assumption that all women want to marry. They sometimes feel that not being married reflects on their attractiveness or personality. Some men find the independence of unmarried women threatening and some married women are envious of their freedom. Our society is geared to couples. Close friendships are not valued or recognized in the same way as marriage. Having to cope alone, make all the decisions and organize your social and working life is an extra reason for needing self-confidence, good support from your friends and widening your horizons.

Self-confidence also helps us to make better partners, refusing to accept bullying behaviour, doing our share of decision-making, and taking more control of our lives. If we feel we have control, it follows that we will be happier and more able to be generous and tolerant. Women with good self-esteem rarely need to manipulate or be aggressive, as they can say what they want and negotiate.

When we are confident, we make more confident mothers.

We can weather our children's rages and set firm boundaries that give them security. We can also gradually let go, share the care of our children with others, and give them greater freedom. A key task for all mothers is to develop their children's self-esteem and bring them up confident, without being stereotyped by gender, but with the good qualities associated with both sexes.

Improved self-esteem also benefits our mental health. We are less likely to suffer from depression, which is often caused by repressed (unexpressed) anger, if we learn to express our anger appropriately and deal with anger from others. We are also less likely to resort to alcohol, drugs or invalidism, and more able to deal with verbal or physical abuse.

Why Christian women?

Women from different cultural and religious backgrounds may experience many of the same problems. However, this book is addressed primarily to Christian women, and the issues it addresses would need to be worked through in a different way in other cultures.

For centuries, Christian women have been taught to model themselves on Mary, the mother of Jesus. We have been taught that she was humble, meek and obedient, as we should be. I believe that Mary was also a strong, assertive woman. Perhaps she has been misunderstood, and was more assertive than we have been taught. She must have been to confront every standard of her synagogue and culture, and take the poverty, oppression and pain that resulted. At the wedding at Cana (John 2.1–10), Jesus seemed reluctant to help with the problem of the shortage of wine, but, presuming he would help in some way, Mary told the servants to obey him. She was not disappointed. Her presence at the cross, to watch her son being tortured, when all the disciples had fled, is an indication of her enormous strength and courage. In St Mark's Chapel in

Jerusalem there is a picture of a strong, middle-aged Jewish woman. According to tradition it is a painting of Mary by St Luke. The Mary it shows is the one who inspires me.

Strength and courage are not the only values we can learn from Mary. The other, more traditional, picture we have is of Mary the Virgin holding the infant Jesus. This also resonates with our own experience and inspires a different side of ourselves. It is an image of exquisite tenderness and love and is mirrored in our own feelings when we hold a baby – our own son or daughter, a grandchild or the child of a friend, a sense of incarnate mystery and infinite possibility. We need to hold on to this loving tenderness and grace as uniquely precious in a world full of conflict, to value and treasure it. In the same way, we need to hold on to our own spiritual hunger and longing for wholeness, nurture and encourage it.

In my experience, many Christian women who have been conditioned for years to believe in their inferiority most need to increase their self-esteem. For centuries women have served others selflessly. They have worked, improvised and sacrificed for their families. When food was short, they went without in order to feed their children and their men. This still happens where there is acute poverty, not just in Third World countries, but here in Britain. This wonderfully unselfish, caring role has sustained many and can give a sense of purpose and satisfaction; a loving sacrifice. What I suggest in this book is not a denial of this role but a better balance, a healthy balance between caring for others and meeting our own needs, developing our own gifts. If our own needs are acknowledged, even if they cannot always be met at once, we can serve others better and without resentment. Perhaps if we can be more aware of the holiness and uniqueness of the people we meet every day, and of the beauty and wonder of the world around us, we may be able to cope more openly and patiently with the difficulties life brings us all.

Many women have accepted the role of martyr for so long that they find it hard to react in any other way. They may sometimes take a masochistic pleasure in it. They have grumbled to friends, talked behind people's backs and denied their own pain without feeling that it is their responsibility to change their situation. By responding differently to discrimination or patronage they could almost certainly have stopped it. If women can grow in self-esteem they can take control of their lives and stop being victims.

Another reason to increase the self-esteem of Christian women is to maximize the contribution they can make to society as a whole. Unless women have the confidence to speak in meetings of all kinds, stand for office in the church and the community, are clear about what changes they want and are prepared to take responsibility, the campaigns of past years, the work started by the suffragettes and continued by the Movement for the Ordination of Women and others, will not continue. It is not just the consolidation of past gains that is at stake. Women are less militaristic than men and our influence in all forms of government can lead to more consultation, more consensus, more compassion and concern about those on the fringes of our communities.

Of course, all women do not want the same thing. We are all different and have diverse ideas about the church and the society we would like to see, but it is important to make our views heard. We need to have the courage to speak for ourselves rather than allow men to put forward what they believe to be our point of view.

Improving your self-esteem is not easy and the habits of a lifetime cannot be transformed in a day but it is taking the first small step which is the most difficult. It may feel foreign, even painful, to begin with, but it is worth persevering, slowly and gently. In this book I suggest many possible ways to start on the road to greater confidence and independence. Although these steps may seem very small, they will lead on, will perhaps lead to the 'more abundant life' (John 10.10) which God intends for us.

First, read this book and see if any of the suggestions appeal to you. Then try some of them, very gently at first. You might like to read more on the subject; if so, other books are listed at the back.

You may also be able to go on an introductory confidence course. There are an increasing number of these short courses available. Ask at your local library or surgery to find out what is being offered. If you have a local Christian Training Scheme, the organizers may be able to help. Or perhaps you have the training or experience to run a course yourself using the material in this book.

Another purpose of this book is to give you some ideas about widening your horizons. I believe that we all live in a tiny piece of the world, in small boxes, surrounded by fences we have erected to keep us safe from anything different, threatening or challenging. We tend to know people like ourselves, eat the same food, do the same things, even holiday in the same place. There are a number of suggestions for enlarging this world in Chapter 9. Try looking at the changes and choices which could expand and enrich your life spiritually as well as socially.

Another way of improving self-esteem is to do some voluntary work. This applies only if you have time to spare. It may be particularly valuable if you have not worked for some years, or have recently retired or been widowed. You may find that this period of voluntary work is only temporary, but it can be a bridge to a place of greater confidence, a sense of direction and even to paid work. There is more about this in Chapter 8.

The next chapter describes some of the reasons why so many of us are under-confident and suggests ways of making improvements.

Chapter 2

— *Valuing Ourselves* —

I ask God . . . to give you power through the Spirit to
be strong in your inner selves.

Ephesians 3.16

Why self-esteem is important

How much we value ourselves profoundly affects every aspect
of our lives. Our love for other people, and the care we are able
to give them, depends on the love we have for ourselves. We
tend to be very aware of our faults and failures but, if we are
reasonably self-confident, we can be free to change these less
useful parts of ourselves. Improved self-esteem can give us the
energy, confidence and improved relationships that enable us
to become all God wants us to be. It is very important.

- Low self-esteem is widespread, especially among women.
  It is not just you!
- Low self-esteem can make us defensive, unable to ask for
  what we want.
- It may make us over-demanding for love and reassurance
  and too dependent on the good opinion of others.
- We may allow ourselves to be treated without respect,
  even with violence.
- We may be unable to say 'no' when we want to, to sex,
  alcohol or drugs.

- It may make us seem aggressive or manipulative when we try to get what we need.
- Because we are so afraid of failing, or being criticized, we may be reluctant to try new things or use our talents to the full.
- We may agree to things because we are afraid to disagree, and fail to stand up for what we know is right.
- We may be devastated by criticism and unable to accept compliments.
- We may not care about our appearance or take proper care of ourselves.

My daughter is a teacher. She had a group of attractive 15-year-old girls for a personal and social skills class. She asked them each to say one thing that they liked about their bodies. Even with encouragement, none of them could think of anything they liked. When asked what they did not like, they named every part of their bodies as too fat, too thin, too big or too small.

What causes low self-esteem?

Childhood experiences

Many reasons for our lack of self-esteem may be rooted in our childhood. As with so many of our problems, it is easy to put the blame on our parents, or whoever brought us up, and there may be good reasons for this. Some people feel that they have never been really loved by their parents and some have been badly damaged by abuse or neglect. If you have suffered badly, assertiveness and confidence-building will not be enough; you need to seek professional help. (There is more about trying to understand your parents in Chapter 7.)

As a child, you may not have had the praise and encouragement all children need. You may have missed out on affection

and care from one or both parents, or been neglected, aban-
doned or orphaned.

Without intending to, our parents, teachers or others may
have damaged our self-confidence. As children, we believed
adults. The things they said to us, or we heard them say to
others, have become part of us. Labels like 'fat', 'plain', 'clumsy'
or 'bossy' may have stuck like burrs, even if they were not
true, or are no longer true. We may have been compared
unfavourably with brothers, sisters or other children or likened
to an unpopular member of the family. Being a girl when a boy
was wanted or expected (or vice versa) can colour the whole of
a childhood.

At school, teachers may have emphasized things that you did
wrong, corrected your mistakes and imposed punishments.
Praise for success is often given only to the few. Passing exams
is often seen as all-important. This leaves many children feeling
they are failures. An elderly woman I know still remembers the
remark on her school report: 'Emily could do better.' This
refrain has been with her all her life, giving her an unjustified
sense of failure.

We may have been teased or bullied because we were different from the other children in some way. Even quite small
things like red hair, wearing glasses or being smaller or fatter
than average can cause misery. If we wore unconventional
clothes, were too clever (or not clever enough), or not good at
games, we may have been scapegoated. Having a different skin
colour may have meant suffering discrimination from teachers
as well as other children. If our parents were different in some
way, or looked different from the other parents, this may have
caused problems, too.

Teasing at school and cruel nicknames may have contributed to our poor self-esteem at a time when we were most
sensitive to the opinion of our peers. I wonder if anyone has
got through their school-days without being picked on for
something? Most of us have survived, but others may still be

affected. It may have taught us to keep our heads down and conform, or it may have made us into rebels.

I can clearly remember when I was six joining in teasing a fat girl at school. I unwisely mentioned this at home. I was taken to my grandmother's room and left in no doubt about the harm I had done. Repentant and tearful, I was desperate to make amends. Granny said I should give the girl something that I treasured to show her I was sorry. The next day I gave her a small wooden dachshund, a recent present. It was a painful lesson.

Experiencing bullying may turn children into bullies themselves. This reaction seems to be more common among boys than among girls. Boys who suffer bullying are more likely to become aggressive, hiding their hurt by taking it out on others. Though girls can and do bully, they may be more likely to turn their aggression inwards; believing they are somehow to blame for being bullied, they take it out on themselves.

As adults, we may still be criticized about our appearance or our efficiency, so it is not surprising that we have got into the habit of thinking of ourselves as full of faults and inadequacies. These feelings are very common, but they are not the only causes of low self-esteem. It may also be caused and reinforced by society.

Women in society

Throughout history, women and men have been treated quite differently by society. Civil rights, like the vote and property rights, have only been granted to women in this century. Until recently, girls were given less education than boys. Women were regarded as being intellectually inferior to men, and when they married, they were seen as the property of their husbands. Women are still paid less than men, on average, and are more likely to be found in part-time, low-paid work.

The essential work of caring for children or the elderly is not regarded as economically important and so receives little acknowledgement or financial reward.

It is not only women who are affected by sexual harassment and domestic and sexual violence, but women are much more likely to be victims. Black and Asian women can find themselves doubly disadvantaged because of racial discrimination in the community and at work. Is it any wonder that so many women still feel of less value than men? It is enshrined in our culture.

Women and the Church

The attitudes of the Church and society have mirrored each other. The average church service is full of reminders that we are selfish, sinful people and unworthy to come before God. We are encouraged to deny ourselves and make more sacrifices in our lives. While this message is important when we are tempted to be self-centred, it is not helpful if we already feel worthless and have low self-esteem. The message most of us need to hear is that God loves and values us as unique, gifted people, made in his image, with a calling to use our gifts in the world.

How we damage our own self-esteem

No one can make you feel inferior without your consent.
Eleanor Roosevelt

Most of us find it easy to put ourselves down; we feed into criticism, agree with negative remarks but reject compliments. We are often our own severest critics, going over and over in our heads the things we wish we had not said or done. Some research suggests that when things go wrong, girls and women are far readier to blame themselves, while boys and men are

more likely to blame the equipment or some other factors outside themselves.

We often play down our own strengths. We find it easy to
say 'I'm not very good at...' but are afraid of being thought
boastful or big-headed if we acknowledge our gifts – a strange
way of being grateful to God for them! Some women set such
high standards for themselves that they cannot live up to them
and then feel guilty and a failure.

On the other hand, if we do gossip unkindly, deliberately
put others down or harm them in some way, we are bound to
damage our own self-esteem. Even if nobody else knows, we
know, and feel guilty.

> Sheila is a wonderfully skilled gardener, imaginative and
> painstaking. When appreciative guests compliment her on
> her beautiful garden, she will point out the solitary dande-
> lion or the small, persistent patch of ground elder. She is not
> just modest, but quite unable to acknowledge her talent, or
> her good fortune, and it is difficult to understand her low
> level of confidence.

Most women I know, especially church women, suffer from
guilt. This is often about what they have not managed to do
rather than from things they have done which they now regret.
These feelings of guilt come from way back; they are 'bred in
the bone'. Women are conditioned to feel guilty. Guilt is so
destructive that it should carry a health warning! If we believe
that God loves us and forgives us, why do we still carry this
burden? Like so many of our burdens, guilt can be eased if we
share it. Some churches encourage confession and absolution
by a priest. If yours does not provide this, find someone to talk
to about your problem who will not belittle your feelings, but
help you work through them and decide what, if anything, you
can do to put it right.

If we try too hard and carry too much we get tired, irritable
and, eventually, ill. If we can value and respect our own needs,

14

we will be able to create a better balance between helping others and caring for ourselves. Loving our neighbour as ourselves must imply that loving ourselves is important.

It is self-defeating to believe that we cannot change, have little control over what happens to us, must be loved or liked by everyone, or that we should not make mistakes. We are human. Mistakes are the way we learn. Our needs and wishes are important and we ignore them at our peril.

How can we improve our self-esteem?

Improving the view we have long had of ourselves is not easy, but we can rely on the help of God, who wants us to grow and change. Increased confidence depends on self-approval, self-care and self-development. It involves learning new skills and being very firm with ourselves. Joining a group to give us support may help.

Self-approval
This means changing the way you talk to yourself:

- Stop blaming yourself. Accept that no one is perfect, but most of the time you try very hard to do the right thing.
- Try not to say, or even think, negative things about yourself.
- Tell yourself: 'I am not to blame for . . .', 'I did my best' or 'I have a right to make mistakes.'
- Acknowledge your achievements, your knowledge and your patience.
- Congratulate yourself on all you have survived (illness, bereavement, unemployment, loss).
- Respect yourself for who you are right now.
- Refuse to be a victim – be a survivor.
- Stop grumbling about the way X treats you. Tackle him or her about it. (See Chapter 4 on giving negative feedback.)

15

- Think positively. You do not need to be perfect.
- If you want something, work for it. Accept the limitations you cannot change. (You may never win Wimbledon, but you could improve your tennis.)
- Be active and learn as much as you can: follow up on what interests you, become an expert in something: knowledge is power.
- Allow yourself to feel proud when you have achieved something: cooked a good meal, handled a difficult situation or made someone laugh, for example.

Fill in the 'What I like about myself' form on pages 18–19 and allow yourself to boast a bit.

Self-care

Looking after yourself better may mean changing your priorities. You may need to give up something so that you can:

- Give yourself more time to rest, exercise or have fun.
- Walk, swim, dance, learn yoga, keep fit, sing, play games, enjoy sex.
- Learn to love and care for your body.
- Take responsibility for your health and get medical help when necessary. Take medicine prescribed.
- Do not abuse drugs or alcohol.
- Eat sensibly and regularly. You will need fewer comfort foods as you begin to feel better about yourself.
- Do what gives you pleasure and satisfaction. Treat yourself with a massage, a sauna or even a long hot bath.
- Be creative, meet new people, learn something new, or take up something you once enjoyed (painting, music, embroidery).

If you find the idea of looking after yourself rather than others immoral, go back to the reasons self-esteem is important. It is not selfish to look after yourself. God made you and values you and loves you. We all need to value our own needs – physical, emotional and spiritual – and give ourselves time and space to grow, to pray and to become all God intends us to be.

We can enlarge our lives and broaden our horizons and that is what this book is about: 'life more abundant'.

Try standing as straight and tall as you can, using as much space as you can, and say:

'I am a strong, loving, gifted woman and God loves me.'

Try this every day, with increasing conviction, until you really believe what you are affirming. You may like to add the name of someone, besides God, who you know loves you.

Self-development
This means getting to know ourselves better and becoming more aware of our reactions and of what we are doing to others, and to ourselves. We need to look at how we relate to other people, especially, perhaps, those we find difficult.

The next section of this book is about learning some of these confidence-building skills. These skills help us to ask for what we want, respect the needs of others, and work out solutions to problems without resorting to aggression or manipulation.

If you begin to practise these skills, your confidence should gradually improve. Most people find it is easier to do this if they have support, so you may find it useful to join a group, or ask a friend to work with you.

Complete the following form by listing some things you like about yourself. If possible, talk to a friend or partner about it and get them to add things they like about you. You may have some surprises!

What I like about myself

I am good at:

....

....

I help others by:

....

....

New friends I have made:

....

....

What I have learned to do for myself (change a tyre, use a word processor, keep accounts):

....

....

Fears I have overcome (shyness, fear of flying):

....

....

I have survived (illness, bereavement, divorce, disability):

....

....

New interests/food/places/skills I have tried:

....

....

A way in which I have grown:

....

....

Support I have been able to ask for:

....

....

Anything else I am proud of:

....

....

Allow yourself to feel proud. Thank God for all the gifts he has given you and all the progress you have made.

Chapter 3

—— *Ways We Behave* ——

When the woman suffering from haemorrhages came up through the crowd and touched Jesus's cloak (Mark 5.25–34), he asked, 'Who touched my clothes?' He dealt with people directly and assertively.

In order to understand some of the skills of confidence-building and some of the choices we have in our behaviour, we need to define the terms that are used. For this purpose, behaviour is divided into four types:

aggressive   indirect   passive   assertive.

We all use all of these ways of behaving at different times. Sometimes aggressive, indirect or passive behaviour may be appropriate, but it is important not to get stuck in any of these modes.

It is important to remember that, as we saw in Chapter 1, the word 'assertive' sounds so like 'aggressive' that the two can be confused. It is aggressive women and men who put others down and frighten them away from church and community organizations, not those who behave assertively.

Aggressive behaviour

Aggressive behaviour involves claiming personal rights and expressing thoughts, feelings and beliefs in a way which interferes with the rights of others. It is characterized by speaking in a loud voice and using intimidating body language: big arm movements, standing too close with head forward, and occupying a lot of space. Aggressive behaviour may be caused by insecurity and a lack of self-esteem, but it can come across as:

- 'This is what I want. What you want is not important'
- rude and inconsiderate
- a totally selfish insistence on getting your own way
- not listening to others, or respecting their opinion
- making yourself appear big, perhaps arrogant
- taking up space, leaving little room for others.

It may make others feel:

- angry
- hurt
- frightened
- humiliated
- defensive
- small
- inadequate
- they want to retaliate or leave.

It will also have an effect on you. Immediately you may:

- feel relief from tension
- feel a sense of power
- get some admiration from others.

In the long term you may:

- feel guilt and shame
- keep wanting to apologize
- blame others
- lose friends and become isolated.

Several years ago my husband and I were having dinner with a number of people we knew only slightly. One of them told an anti-Semitic joke. Most people laughed. I was really angry and said, loudly and aggressively, 'That joke is racist and not funny.' There was a pregnant silence. Then everyone started talking at once. At the time I felt good, like a crusader on a charger, but now I see how rude I was. If I had said it gently but assertively, it might have been effective. Whether my response resulted in that person giving up racist jokes, I have no way of telling. We were never asked again.

In some circumstances, aggression in expressing a passionate conviction, or preventing injustice, may be inevitable and may convert others. But it may also frighten them or make them angry. Either reaction can have negative effects in the long run.

Aggressive women can be very frightening to men as well as women, as can aggressive men but, unlike women, men are not labelled 'strident', 'bossy', or 'feminist'. We need to develop ways of being strong, positive and powerful by being assertive rather than aggressive.

Caroline was a powerful woman who chaired the parish council and controlled much of the communal life of the village. She was efficient and effective and, in some ways, admirable. But she was impatient with other people's shortcomings and often blunt to the point of rudeness. Convinced that she knew best, she often won her battles, but she made some people very angry and terrified others.

If she had been a man, Caroline's aggressiveness would have been more acceptable. She would probably have been called a strong leader and her achievements acclaimed. Perhaps both women and men find controlling women like Caroline threatening because they remind them of how all-powerful their mothers seemed when they were very young.

Indirect or manipulative behaviour

This is often used by women when dealing with men. It gives the message 'I'm going to get what I want, without you knowing.' It can involve:

- being unable to ask directly for what you want
- making others feel guilty
- sulking, sarcasm, or silence
- deliberately using tears to get what you want
- ignoring the other person or trying to get your own way indirectly
- using sex as a weapon.

It may make others feel:

- uncomfortable
- threatened
- manipulated
- angry
- unable to trust you.

It may give you:

- a sense of power
- an opportunity to hide your real feelings and avoid confrontation.

But in the long term you may feel:

- inadequate and immature
- angry or guilty that you have not been more direct
- frustrated when the other person does not get the message.

This behaviour may be used when you are insecure or under pressure. It may be effective, but it undermines trust and can backfire.

23

Eleanor, an attractive, intelligent woman, was married to George, a domineering, demanding husband and successful journalist, who insisted on constant attention and criticized her for any flaw in her appearance or her housekeeping. He was devoted to her and dependent on her. The only way that Eleanor could meet her own needs, or have any say in what happened, was by using indirect, manipulative behaviour. While apparently passive and obedient, and expert at hiding her real feelings, she kept information from George, used half-truths and other small deceptions. If she ever directly stated what she wanted, she met with ridicule, so she learned to pretend that it was what someone else had asked for or suggested. This strategy was usually successful, but it became a habit and, when George died, Eleanor had difficulty in relating to other people more openly.

Eleanor's behaviour was the way she could cope with George's demands. She was not conscious of being manipulative. If she had been able to be more assertive early in her marriage, the relationship might not have satisfied George's need to dominate and might therefore have ended in divorce.

Passive behaviour

This gives the message 'What I want does not count. My feelings do not matter.' Hunched shoulders, a small voice, lowered head, avoidance of eye contact, small hand movements and arms hugging the body are all typical of passive behaviour.

Because it reflects a failure honestly to express your feelings, thoughts and beliefs, it shows a lack of respect for your own needs and your own abilities. You express yourself in such an apologetic, self-effacing manner that other people can ignore you. Passive behaviour may be confused with humility in the biblical sense, and some men approve of it in women.

It may be due to:

24

- a desire to please
- low self-esteem
- fear of the consequences of more assertive behaviour
- wanting to appease others.

It often involves

- constant apologies for your actions and opinions
- expressing your ideas in such a self-effacing way that other people disregard them
- not standing up for your rights and allowing others to take advantage of you
- saying yes when you mean no
- denying some of your God-given gifts.

In the short term, passive behaviour may make you feel helpful or good because you have avoided conflict. You may prefer to call it humility.

In the long term, it may:

- make you feel like a victim of injustice, resentful and angry
- leave you feeling ineffectual and of no account
- lead to even lower self-esteem, hurt, anger and self-pity
- tempt you to take out your feelings on someone even more vulnerable than yourself
- become a habit, the line of least resistance, and a refusal to make your own decisions.

Sue had behaved passively most of her life. She was a small, quiet, rather dowdy woman whose husband, Ron, was often away on business. They had three grown-up sons. Sue was hard-working and self-effacing; she always seemed to be apologizing. She had spent years at the beck and call of Ron and the boys and even her sharp little terrier seemed to get his own way with her. Married young, she had never had a job outside her home. A few years ago Ron had to

25

work abroad for six months. Her sons were busy with their wives and babies. As she had time on her hands and seemed rather lost, she was asked to be secretary of the church council. It took a lot of persuasion to convince her that she could do the job and at first she needed support and reassurance. Gradually her confidence grew as she discovered a new strength and ability. One outward sign of her greater self-esteem was the dramatic improvement in her appearance. What Ron said when he returned is not known. It must have been hard for him to adjust to his 'new' wife, but they are still happily married. Sue is no longer secretary of the council as she has a responsible, full-time job.

This is a good example of how, by overcoming initial fears and deciding to take on a new challenge, someone's passive life-style can be changed, new talent discovered and choices broadened. It seems that Ron was mature and secure enough to adapt to a wife who had gained in confidence. Not all men would be able to do this as readily and it may take a combination of tact, firmness and negotiation to persuade them.

Assertive behaviour

Assertive behaviour is characterized by standing tall, shoulders back but relaxed, direct eye contact and a calm, clear voice.

Assertiveness is an attitude of mind which involves:

- developing a belief and confidence in yourself and your talents
- becoming more aware of the emotions which influence the decisions you make and how you come across to other people
- trying to make your communication with others as simple, open and honest as possible
- actively listening, showing you understand and respect the other person

26

- not scoring points or putting others down
- recognizing your own needs and asking directly for what you want
- ensuring that messages are clear and relationships open.

You are on a long train journey and have deliberately chosen a non-smoking compartment. A woman lights a cigarette. What do you do?

- Put up with it?
- Ostentatiously open a window?
- Complain loudly to your companion?
- Say angrily 'This is not a smoking compartment'?
- Sigh, cough deliberately, or 'look daggers'?
- Ask them politely but firmly not to smoke?

Which response is most likely to be effective in getting the woman to stop smoking?

Behaving assertively:

- gives you a sense of being in control and responsible for your actions
- is more likely to solve problems
- makes communication more effective
- enables you to make decisions
- causes less stress
- maintains and improves your self-esteem
- resolves differences, allows for compromise and enables joint solutions to be negotiated
- does not necessarily ensure that you get what you want.

The effect on others is that:

- they feel listened to, valued and appreciated
- they can trust you to be honest, even when you are being critical

- they respect and trust you, even if they disagree with you
- problem-solving becomes more straightforward.

If you were planning a church fête, who would you prefer to deal with?

- Someone who shouts you down and always knows best?
- Someone who hints and never comes to the point?
- Someone who says 'I don't mind' when you know they do?
- Someone who respects your authority and clearly explains their ideas for you to accept or reject?

On the following pages more detail is given about how to behave assertively in different situations. We are all different, not only in age, culture and life-style, but in temperament. Some people find it more difficult to be assertive in some situations, at home perhaps, or at work. If this behaviour is very foreign to you, start slowly and see what effect it has on other people and on yourself. Even quite small steps can make a difference.

Mrs Thomas went to her GP to ask for tranquillizers. She had been on them for years for stress, but with the doctor's encouragement had cut them down to one a day, taken at tea-time. When the doctor asked why she needed one at tea-time, she explained that when her husband and her son came home they never agreed about whether they should have chips or mashed potato for tea that day, so she always ended up having to make both. She found this very annoying. The doctor suggested that she should give them chips one day and mash the next and tell them firmly what she was going to do. This simple arrangement worked wonderfully and also gave Mrs Thomas the courage to be more assertive in other areas. She no longer needed tranquillizers.

Chapter 4

— A Confident Answer —

Just then a Canaanite woman from that region came out and started shouting, 'Have mercy on me, Lord, Son of David, my daughter is tormented by a demon.' But he did not answer her at all. And his disciples came and urged him, saying, 'Send her away, for she keeps shouting after us.' He answered, 'I was sent only to the lost sheep of the house of Israel.' But she came and knelt before him, saying, 'Lord, help me.' He answered, 'It is not fair to take the children's food and throw it to the dogs.' 'Yes, Lord, yet even the dogs eat the crumbs that fall from their master's table.' Then Jesus answered her, 'Woman, great is your faith! Let it be done for you as you wish.' And her daughter was healed instantly.

Matthew 15.22–28

Making requests

The Canaanite woman not only asked for what she wanted, but had the courage to argue with Jesus, and to argue with wit. If she was offended by his first response, she did not let that get in the way. She persisted. Jesus responded to her assertiveness.

Because of our low self-esteem and fear of rejection, many of us avoid asking for what we need or want. Somewhere, deep down, we believe that we are not worth the attention or help of others. Asking for help is especially difficult, as it seems to

29

reinforce our sense of inadequacy. We feel feeble because we cannot manage on our own. We believe that we ought to be strong and self-sufficient. So we often do not get the help we need because we are afraid to ask.

If we want agreement to a plan, promotion at work, or to offer our help, for example, it takes an enormous effort even to mention it. What is meant to be a request comes out as a hint, or very tentative suggestion, just asking to be refused or ignored. We may begin by apologizing for mentioning it, putting ourselves in the other person's debt for even listening to us!

If, on the other hand, someone asks us for our help we usually feel pleased and rather flattered. It is warming to think that we can be of use, and good for our self-esteem. Is it lack of confidence that prevents us from offering help when we would like to? Sometimes we would really like to help, but fear of rejection holds us back.

> Joyce was an old friend of our family. Unmarried, she was eccentric and fiercely independent. After her visits we would drop her at a tube station. 'Don't get out,' she would say. 'I'll soon find someone to help with my bag.' She approached the next able-bodied man who came along and went into the station with him carrying her suitcase. It never seemed to fail. She got the help she needed with a mixture of charm and assertiveness.

We have a right to ask for what we want or offer help. The other person has a right to refuse. To make a request in an assertive way:

- do not apologize
- be brief and direct
- give a reason if it helps
- do not oversell or go into long explanations
- do not hint or ask indirectly

- take the responsibility; do not hide behind someone else.

This direct, open approach shows the other person where you stand and enables them to agree or disagree openly and with the least possible damage to your relationship. It increases respect.

Jesus was able to ask for what he wanted clearly and directly. In Mark 11.2–6 he says:

'Go to the village opposite, and, as you enter, you will find tethered there a colt which no one has yet ridden. Untie it and bring it here. If anyone asks, "Why are you doing that?" say, "Our Master needs it, and will send it back without delay".'

Saying no

If making a request is difficult, saying no is even more so. The difficulty is our fear of being thought selfish, uncaring or insensitive to the needs of others. It is part of the human condition to mind what people think of us and women are often especially vulnerable to this. We genuinely want to be kind and generous, but are unsure where the limits are, or even whether there should be limits to our generosity or our time. Some people feel that it is hard to reconcile the gospel message of unconditional love with setting realistic limits, but we do know that if we over-stretch ourselves and take on more than we can cope with, we become exhausted, irritable and, eventually, ill. This cannot be God's will for us.

If you are not sure what you should do:

- Listen to your immediate gut reaction as it is the best guide to whether you should say yes or no.
- Ask for time to think about it.
- Think about the effect your decision will have on you and others.
- Pray about it.

- Don't allow yourself to be blackmailed by emotional pressure, manipulation or anger – it is your choice.
- Ask for more information ('I don't know. I need more information').

If you have decided to say no:

- Keep your reply brief, avoid excuses, especially dishonest ones.
- Say 'No', clearly and directly. You may need to say it more than once.
- Look the other person in the eye.
- Don't keep apologizing; once is enough.
- Accept that your refusal may annoy or inconvenience them.
- Offer a compromise if you want to, but avoid making promises for the future unless you really mean them.
- Acknowledge the other person's feelings ('I can see this will cause you difficulties'). You are rejecting the request, not the person. Make this clear.
- Negotiate, if appropriate. ('I will . . . if you will . . . .')
- If you really want to, say 'I will this time, but not again.' But do stick to it!

It will help the other person if you are clear and direct, because they won't be tempted to keep up the pressure to make you change your mind.

Remember, you have a right to say no without feeling guilty.

Anne's friend Sally was always asking her for help with baby-sitting, cutting her hair or getting her shopping. Anne had problems of her own and resented these constant requests, but did not like to refuse. So she delayed answering until she plucked up the courage to say no, saying she would have to look in her diary and would let Sally know. When Anne's self-esteem had improved, she was able to say no at once and also to discuss with Sally the help she needed and what Anne could happily offer. This made her feel less guilty and enabled Sally to understand how dependent she had become.

Try not to say no to new tasks or experiences just because you have never done them before. If you think you cannot do it, offer to learn how. Perhaps this request is a new challenge and you should give up something else to make time to do it. It is your choice.

Church life can be full of traditions, the same people doing the same things year after year – 'But you always run the tombola!' This puts pressure on the few active people and excludes others who might like to be asked. If we have done the same task for years it is easy to believe that no one else can do it as well.

The broken record

This is one technique you can use to say no, ask a question or make a complaint. You keep repeating the same phrase over and over again as if the needle was stuck on an old-fashioned record. For example, say you take an appliance back to the shop because it does not work. You want your money back. The shopkeeper offers to repair it or replace it, but you keep repeating 'I would like my money back, please. It does not work, I want my money back.' If you keep this up, it usually works. But beware, it can be very irritating!

Years ago our MP gave a talk in our church about the need for nuclear weapons. Afterwards I asked him, 'In what circumstances do you think we should use nuclear weapons?' He replied, 'You shouldn't bother your pretty little head about things like that.'

What did I do or say? To my shame, nothing! At first I fell for the 'pretty little head' and felt flattered, but, almost immediately, felt patronized and furious. I wish I had ignored his remark and just politely repeated the question using the 'broken record' method until he was forced to answer.

Receiving criticism

When other people say no to us it is easy to take it as criticism. Criticism makes us feel rejected and vulnerable and damages our self-esteem. In order to learn from it and use it to grow, we need to be able to deal with it in a constructive way, discriminating between valid, unclear and invalid criticism. We can then react more positively and use it to help us change.

When you receive criticism, it is important to clarify what has been said and then decide whether it is true or untrue. Remember, it is their opinion. You may need to check it with someone else. Always try to empathize with the other person and understand how it feels to them.

Unclear criticism

If you are not quite sure what they are getting at, ask them to explain exactly what they mean: 'What is it that...?' Use 'What', not 'Why' to keep the focus on your behaviour rather than on their motives for criticizing you.

- Listen carefully.
- Repeat back what has been said and clarify it ('So what you are saying is . . .').
- Ask for more ('Is there anything else that I need to look at?').
- Disagree assertively where their facts are wrong, but not with their opinions.
- Problem-solve or negotiate ('I will . . . if you will . . .').
- The criticism may have more to do with their state of mind than with you.

Valid criticism

This is criticism which you know to be true and may be useful to you. If you decide that the other person's criticism is valid, thank them.

If you have made a mistake:

- admit it openly – 'Yes, I did forget to do that'
- say sorry once and mean it; don't over-apologize
- don't counter-attack ('But you make mistakes too')
- recognize the other person's feelings ('I realize that you are annoyed')
- look to the future and avoiding a recurrence ('I'll try not to do that in future')
- be aware of your extreme sensitivity to particular criticisms – your 'crumple buttons' (see below).

Crumple buttons

These may go back to your childhood, to names you were called, perhaps. You may feel totally thrown or defeated by one specific criticism, lose your temper or burst into tears. If you recognize these triggers you may be more able to control yourself.

> My particular 'crumple button' is the word 'bossy'. I was frequently called this as a child. I had a fairly amenable younger sister and I did direct our games and take the plum parts in our acting. I was always the pirate captain and she was the cabin boy! I can now see that I was a natural leader, but needed to learn to use this skill less aggressively. My horror of the label 'bossy' in later life sometimes meant that I avoided leadership positions and this affected my career.

Invalid criticism

These are comments which you believe to be untrue. Ask someone you trust to be honest and to tell you if the criticism is true or if it is something to do with the person who criticized you. It could be that envy is the real reason for their criticism.

If you decide the criticism is invalid:

- listen carefully, keeping calm and neutral but firm
- show the other person that you understand how they are feeling ('I realize that you feel hurt/upset, but . . .')
- when it is important, reply assertively that you do not agree, using the same words that they used ('I do not agree at all, I am not . . .')
- give a reason for your opinion without becoming defensive
- decide if the issue is important enough to take up; if it is not, try 'fogging', being deliberately vague ('Perhaps I did . . .' or 'Yes, I recognize that you feel . . .').

Receiving compliments

Each man should examine his own conduct for himself; then he can measure his achievement by comparing himself with himself and not with anyone else.

Galatians 6.4

So often we compare ourselves with others and so feel inadequate. In our culture we are not good at accepting compliments. There is no accepted way of doing it. Americans usually smile and say 'Thank you'. We are often afraid of being thought 'big-headed' and so appear to reject the gift of a compliment. We may brush it off or deny it: 'I only did part of it, Judy helped me,' 'I bought it at Oxfam for 50p.'

In spite of any possible embarrassment, our suspicion of ulterior motives (What do they want?) and our need for modesty, we need to learn to accept compliments by:

- smiling and looking the other person in the eye

- thanking them ('Thank you, I'm glad you like it,' 'I'm pleased that you thought so,' 'I like this colour too').

It is important to accept and believe compliments. If we reject or devalue them, the giver will feel devalued or put down. If necessary, ask for clarification: 'It would be useful for me to know what you meant by "You have been so helpful." In what way did I help?'

Compliments increase goodwill and self-esteem. They make everyone feel better. We all need many more of them!

Fiona was the efficient manager of a works canteen but had always suffered from low self-esteem. She attended a confidence course. The suggestions about compliments struck a chord with her. She realized that she rejected the compliments she did receive, always giving the credit to someone else or thinking she was just being 'buttered up'. So, at the suggestion of the course tutor, she decided to keep a record of all the nice things people said to her. She bought a small red notebook, in which she entered the compliments she received and any positive remarks made to her. At the end of six months, at a course reunion, she proudly showed the book. She had quite a collection of positive comments to reread when she felt low. Her self-esteem had improved immeasurably. She could recognize how much support she had received and was also more able to praise and support the other workers at the canteen.

Sometimes quite a small effort to recognize our own value brings about positive changes.

Making constructive criticisms

Criticism can teach us more about ourselves and the effect our behaviour has on others. Constructive feedback can increase self-awareness and encourage development. It is important to learn to give and receive it. Negative feedback, given skilfully, can be very important and useful, a valuable gift. But it is important to try to be aware of our own prejudices and projections. In spite of his chauvinism, Lord Byron puts it well:

> As soon
> Seek roses in December, ice in June;
> Hope constancy in wind, or corn in chaff;
> Believe a woman or an epitaph,
> Or any other thing that's false, before
> You trust in critics, who themselves are sore
> from 'English Bards and Scotch Reviewers'

- Try to time your criticisms well. Consider carefully when and where to make them (not too long after the event).
- Check with the other person that it is a convenient time to talk.
- Start with something positive. Tell them what you like or admire about them first and they will be more likely to receive the negative feedback.
- As a rule, people need to hear three good things to one bad if they are to grow.
- Be clear about the behaviour you are criticizing; do not generalize or label. For example, don't say 'I think you are a domineering person,' but 'I felt really threatened when you said . . .'.
- Select priority areas that need changing instead of presenting them with a huge bumper pack of faults.
- Refer to behaviour which can be modified. Don't tell people they are 'too old' or 'too young', for example.
- Offer alternatives, positive suggestions about how to behave differently.
- Be descriptive. Tell the person the effect their behaviour had on you.
- Own the feedback. Begin with 'I' or 'In my opinion', not 'Everyone thinks . . .'.

- Leave the recipient a choice whether to change or not.
- Problem-solve, look to the future, negotiate, be positive.
- Say what you would like (e.g. 'Please would you . . .').

Giving feedback constructively is a gift. *Give more* of it.

This straightforward, honest approach is much more likely to enable the person to change, without hurting them too much. If we store up resentment, we may eventually explode with anger and frustration and say more than we intend, causing damage and a soured relationship.

Chapter 5

— Anger and Assertiveness —

Again he entered the synagogue and a man was there who had a withered hand. They watched him to see whether he would cure him on the sabbath, so that they might accuse him. And he said to the man who had the withered hand, 'Come forward.' Then he said to them, 'Is it lawful to do good or to do harm on the sabbath, to save life or to kill?' But they were silent. He looked around at them with anger; he was grieved at their hardness of heart and said to the man, 'Stretch out your hand.' He stretched it out, and his hand was restored.

Mark 3.1–5

Dealing with our own anger

This is a difficult subject, as the causes of our anger can range from insensitive criticism to frustration or abuse. It is also difficult because most women, perhaps especially older ones, are afraid of their anger. We have been conditioned to believe that anger is not acceptable in women. It is seen as 'unfeminine'. 'Angry young men' (or even angry old ones) are culturally acceptable. Angry women, on the other hand, may be labelled 'hysterical' or 'harridans'.

Our own anger can be frightening, because we are afraid of losing control of ourselves and of our own potential for violence. Those who rouse most anger in us are often those closest to us, our parents, partners, children or close friends.

This can make us feel acutely guilty. We still love the people who make us angry but the intensity of our feelings may terrify us.

What often happens is that we deny and hide these feelings, 'repress' them, as psychologists would say. It seems to be generally accepted by doctors that repressed anger leads to depression. A large proportion of women have experienced depression at some time in their lives and know how disabling it can be. So dealing with anger by accepting responsibility for it is important, as is learning to express it constructively.

If we can face and acknowledge the real cause of our anger, we can use it creatively. It can be a source of energy. Try:

- saying 'I feel very angry'
- releasing the physical tension by taking a few deep breaths, walking fast, hitting a pillow or 'strangling' a towel
- discharging the emotion by crying or shouting, preferably when alone
- writing down how angry you feel, then destroying what you have written (letters that are sent in this mood are almost always regretted later)
- talking to someone you trust not to fuel your anger and trying to identify the real cause of it
- giving a clear message about what change you want from the person who has made you angry; try to talk in terms of their behaviour – do not label the person.

Be aware that your anger may really be about something in your past, and has simply been sparked off by this situation.

Projected anger

The object of anger is not always its real cause. For example, something upsets you at work and you take it out on your family. A mother hits a child in the street because she felt insulted by a shop assistant's remark. This is sometimes called 'projected anger'. It is the result of repressing, or hiding, our anger rather than being aware of it and dealing with it directly.

Naomi was a caring young mother who loved her two-year-old twin sons dearly. One day, when looking for a space in the car park, a large car backed out without seeing her, hit her rear bumper, smashing the lights, and drove away. Naomi was furious, but there seemed nothing she could do. She and the twins went to the supermarket. The boys noisily demanded sweets and, to keep them quiet, she gave them some Smarties. By the time they reached the check-out, Naomi was tired and stressed and forgot to declare the Smarties to the cashier. Challenged about this rather aggressively, and afraid of being accused of dishonesty, she pretended that the boys had taken the sweets without her permission and, to their bewilderment, smacked them both hard. This seemed to prove her innocence and satisfied the cashier. But, of course, the twins howled in pain and outrage.

If Naomi had been able to express her anger to the car driver, and had had the energy to be more assertive with the cashier, her anger need not have been taken out on the little boys.

We have all been on the receiving end of projected anger. There may have been an outburst triggered by a mildly irritating remark we made, but the real cause was something completely different. We may be left bemused and resentful unless we can trace the underlying cause of the anger.

Once, when my children were young, I arrived home from a difficult day at work to find their coats and school things all over the floor. Feeling tired and cross, I told them off. My younger son, then aged nine, followed me into the kitchen and said: 'Mum, why do you have this neurotic need to overwork?' At the time I could cheerfully have strangled him, but, of course, there was some truth in what he said and he certainly recognized projected anger at an early age!

Constructive anger

There are times when anger, a very basic emotion, is necessary. We need the energy and power that anger gives us if we are to act against injustice, violence or poverty. Jesus himself got angry at people who were intolerant and put adhering to the law before relieving suffering, as in the passage from St Mark quoted at the beginning of this chapter.

There are many things in the world to make us angry, even where we are not personally involved and, if we are 'members one of another' (Ephesians 4.25), often it is surely right to be angry. We may feel angry when we see or read about homelessness, child abuse or environmental pollution, for example. This kind of anger can be channelled constructively. We are not powerless. We can change things. Alone we can make a difference. Together we can change the world.

- We can write letters to our MP, to government departments and to newspapers. (Amnesty International has proved how effective this can be in getting political prisoners released or their treatment improved.)
- We can join, or subscribe to, voluntary organizations dealing with the problem that concerns us (the NSPCC, Shelter or Greenpeace, for example).
- We can find the courage to go to political meetings and ask questions.
- If we care enough, we can join demonstrations. (The demonstrations against the Poll tax were very effective.)
- We can use our vote, and help campaign, at parliamentary and local elections.

Our anger will be more effective if we use it assertively rather than aggressively. It will help improve our society and make it more caring.

Anger is one of the sinews of the soul.

Thomas Fuller (1608-1661)

43

Dealing with anger from others

If someone is angry with you, it can be very frightening and may make you feel sick and shaky. Anger is also very infectious and, if someone really goes for you, you can find yourself getting equally angry. It is a defensive instinct to want to reply angrily if you feel attacked, or hit back if you are hit.

If you can contain your anger by expressing how you feel – 'I feel furious when you say that' – it may avoid a confrontation in which you say things you will later regret. Not losing your temper will put you in a strong negotiating position. Although you may want to escape from the anger, it may be better to stand your ground and see it through.

If you want to deal with the problem assertively, and can keep calm enough, try to:

- recognize the other person's anger ('I can see that you are really angry')
- establish eye contact (unless you think they may become violent)
- listen to what they are saying and try to understand
- clarify what they are saying
- repeat their name, or say 'Listen to me' until you have their attention
- speak quietly so that they have to stop shouting to hear you
- state your views firmly, if it seems appropriate
- if they are too unreasonable, say 'We will talk about it later,' and leave
- avoid arguing
- keep your distance.

If violence is threatened, leave. (There is more about domestic violence in Chapter 7.)

Chapter 6

Loving Ourselves As —— *Our Neighbour* ——

You shall love your neighbour as yourself.

Matthew 19.19

We cannot fully love other people unless we love and respect ourselves. For most of us it is harder to love ourselves than to love others. Loving ourselves does not mean being selfish or always expecting to have our own way. It means not running ourselves down, but valuing our gifts, and respecting our uniqueness. It also means, I think, not letting our pride prevent us from asking for and accepting help when we need it.

The following way of defining how we feel and react at different times, and the quotes with each section, are taken from the well-known book *I'm OK, You're OK* by Thomas A. Harris. How we are feeling directly affects how we behave to other people. We all experience the whole range of feelings at some time, but how we are most of the time is what is important.

I'm not OK, you're OK is described by Harris as:

the universal position of early childhood; being the infant's logical conclusion from the situation of birth and infancy . . . The child, by virtue of his small size and helplessness, inevitably considers himself inferior to the adult figures in his environment.

45

So we may have remained in this position since early child-hood, having low self-esteem and comparing ourselves unfavourably with others. When we feel like this we may behave passively, believing that everything must be our fault, and barely daring to express an opinion let alone saying what we would like for ourselves. This is the attitude of abused wives and often of bullied children. Many women get stuck in this way of behaving and even seem quite proud of it. We may justify it as a kind of humility. We all feel like this sometimes, but if you are often in this position you may need to work at improving your sense of self-worth and get more help and support.

> 'That was a delicious meal! You are such a wonderful cook. I am so hopeless. I just can't seem to follow recipes.'

I'm not OK, you're not OK according to Harris:

> A person in this position gives up. There is no hope. He simply gets through life . . .

This is when we feel really depressed and hopeless. We may move to one of the other positions as the way out. Again if you feel like this too often and for too long you need to think about getting help.

> 'I can't work this machine. You are no good at it either. Let's give up.'

I'm OK, you're not OK Harris describes people in this position as:

> They are the persons without a conscience who are con-vinced that they are OK no matter what they do and that the total fault in every situation lies in others.

We are in this position if we feel self-righteous and do not accept responsibility for our problems, or if someone has let us down badly and we are full of criticism and condemnation of them. If we can remind ourselves that the other person is 'OK', not entirely hopeless, we may begin to look at the reasons they have let us down, or perhaps even wonder if it was partly our fault. Was our communication with them clear?

> 'It's a pity your hair always looks such a mess. You should try my hairdresser, she does mine so well.'

I'm OK, you're OK is when we treat others with respect and also value ourselves. This attitude allows us to agree or disagree with others and helps us to accept differences without feeling that either we or they are wrong. It makes us comfortable and confident. It is from this positive position that we can move forward and negotiate solutions. When we feel like this we can act assertively.

> 'Look at our children, playing so well together, don't they look happy and healthy. I reckon we must both be doing a good job as Mums.'

Harris says:

> The first three (positions) are unconscious, having been made early in life . . . The fourth position 'I'm OK, you're OK' is a conscious and verbal decision . . . We do not drift into a new position. It is a decision we make. In this respect it is like a conversion experience.

I have found the following diagram helpful in understanding these positions and how, if we can be aware of which box we are in at any time, we can consciously decide to move from one position to another. Try to move into the last position as much as possible. This may be especially important if you want to tackle a difficult situation, say no to a request, or criticize someone's behaviour. However angry you feel it is important to remember 'they are OK, and so am I.' Try to be aware of which box you are in.

The moral is: it is not possible to love our neighbour unless we also love ourselves.

I'm not OK You're OK (Passive)	I'm not OK You're not OK (Depressive)
I'm OK You're not OK (Aggressive)	I'm OK You're OK (Assertive)

Getting support

Even men and women with a good sense of self-worth need support when faced with special difficulties. Having to cope with bereavement, life-threatening illness, redundancy, disability, divorce or violence can mean that we need the love, concern and objectivity of someone outside the situation to help us survive and cope.

If you have low self-esteem, you may find it difficult to ask for the help and support you need because you believe that you are not worth anyone's time or attention. But this is a catch-22 situation, for, unless you get the support, your confidence will not improve. We are social beings and, though our needs vary, we can only flourish if we have the affection and concern of others and a sense of solidarity with them.

As I said earlier, if you want to change and improve your sense of self-worth, you will need the help of your family, friends, a group or perhaps a professional counsellor. No one can cope alone all the time. It is no reflection on you: we all need support and should help others to give it to us. Not to ask for help when we need it is a kind of pride, perhaps the only kind of pride that afflicts women. 'I can manage,' we say, and so deprive others of the pleasure of feeling needed. We do not mean to put ourselves on a pedestal, but that is the impression we can sometimes give.

Sources of help

Try not to rely on only one person. They may die, move away or not always be able to help. Use different people for different kinds of support. Think about who helped you in the past. At first it may be hard to ask another person for help, but remember how pleased you have been to be asked for your help. Extending your contacts and circle of friends will open up more possible sources of help.

There are also many different agencies who are there to help: Cruse, Gingerbread, Relate and the Samaritans are just a few examples. You can get their phone numbers from the library or Citizens Advice Bureau. Macmillan nurses or counsellors are attached to some surgeries to help patients cope with life-threatening diagnosis and bereavement. There are, in most areas, a range of 'alternative' practitioners – acupuncturists, healers, aromatherapists and others – who may be the answer for you. Talk to your doctor about sources of help.

Groups

Joining a women's group can be an enormous help. It might be a church women's group, a house group or a community one. A group working on personal development is likely to be the most productive, but any group where members have the opportunity to share some aspect of their lives is valuable. You may have a number of friends or neighbours who would welcome the chance to meet regularly over a cup of tea. Could you start your own group for mutual support?

Joan and her husband Bob were shattered when their longed-for first baby, Zoe, was born with Down's syndrome.

It seemed like the end of the world. For 24 hours they could not bear to see her. With their agreement, a social worker came to see them in the hospital and then at home. She helped them express their guilt, anger and sense of irretrievable loss and enabled them to support each other. Zoe was very appealing and their love for her grew. In a few months they were ready to meet other parents, in a group, to mourn with them and rejoice over the progress of their babies. This support enabled them to survive.

Giving support

Most women give support to someone, a family member, friend or colleague. You may already be involved in counselling as part of your job, or as a member of your church. Even if you are feeling low, you can still help someone else. It is often by sharing our doubts and failures that we encourage others to share theirs. Many women, even those with low self-esteem, are good, sympathetic listeners and can often acknowledge this strength while recognizing few others.

For example, since it has become known that I have had breast cancer, several women who have just had it diagnosed, or are too afraid to admit to their doctor that they have a lump, have been prepared to talk to me about it. Because it is such a difficult illness to face up to, and one needs so much support, I have found it helpful not to keep it secret, but we all cope in different ways.

Rosemary, a woman with low self-esteem, was anxious about a coming interview with her daughter's headmistress. She described the head as rather unsympathetic and abrupt. After discussing her fears, I suggested that we practise the interview. I would be the headmistress and she would practise what she wanted to say to me. We started quite well, and I was enjoying acting the abrupt head, when Rosemary burst into tears, saying 'you don't usually talk to me like that, Jennifer.' She had not fully understood that I was just pretending. I have been more careful about acting since then! The real interview went quite well and the head proved less fierce than I had been.

Here are a few guidelines to increase the effectiveness of your help, which you may be already aware of, but are worth a reminder:

- Keep anything you are told in confidence strictly confidential.
- Listen carefully to what the other person says.
- Try not to give advice.
- It may be helpful to share your experience briefly, but do not interrupt the flow of their story with long anecdotes about your own problems. Remember, your solution may not be theirs. They need to find their own answers.
- Encourage them to talk by asking 'How did you feel?' Repeat what they said, using their words, and ask them to say more.
- Encourage them to think about the other side of the problem too ('How do you think he felt about it?').
- If they are criticizing someone, you should not add fuel to the flames by adding your own criticism, but nor should you defend them.

What is important is for the person you are listening to to feel free to express their fears and their feelings without being judged or criticized. This in itself is healing and often enables them to see a solution.

Encourage them to look at their options for the future:

What outcome they would like.
What the alternatives are.
What action they can take.

- If you disagree with their decisions, remember that it is their choice.
- Build up their self-esteem by stressing their strengths.
- Show them that you care about them and sympathize with them without necessarily agreeing with them.
- Pray for them and tell them that you are, if it is appropriate.
- Follow up by phoning to ask how they are, without pushing for a sequel.
- If they are threatening, or even talking about harming themselves or other people they need professional help. You should firmly suggest that they see their doctor.

As a social worker, I often felt overwhelmed and helpless in the face of other people's agonizing circumstances. Sometimes all I could do was listen, pray for them, show them my concern and lend them my hope that they would survive. Sharing their despair seemed healing in itself. Other people have done this for me at bad moments and I am grateful to them.

If you feel overstretched or exhausted, do not feel you always have to go on helping others. We all have our limits. Say 'No, not now'.

Jesus often withdrew to the wilderness, as in Matthew 14.23:

And after he had dismissed the crowds, he went up the mountain by himself to pray. When evening came he was there alone.

We too may sometimes need to be alone, away from the demands of others.

Young people may be especially in need of someone other than their parents who is willing and able to listen to them. Their self-esteem may be very fragile. Be careful to encourage rather than criticize.

Supporting and encouraging other women at work and in the Church is very important. So often it is other women who undermine us, not in the same way that men do, but more subtly. What we see as our strengths may be stumbling-blocks for others. Our efficiency, for example, may make others feel inadequate. I know that my enthusiasm has often put others off the cause I am advocating but, used more gently, it can enthuse and enable others.

We encourage others to discover their abilities when we ask for their help, encourage their ideas and trust them. If you have a position of any authority in your church or at work, use it to support, encourage and promote other women. Build their self-esteem by recognizing and praising their work and their talent. If they are younger, more attractive or more intelligent than you, you may feel threatened. Be confident about your own strengths, but be generous and helpful; they may be more insecure than they seem. Do not imitate men's style of leadership. Be yourself. Women are often better at encouraging co-operation and consensus.

When I was a young child care officer, I felt overwhelmed by the responsibility of placing children in foster homes or for adoption. How could one know if it was going to be right? A Catholic colleague told me, 'You do everything you can, references, checks, use your intuition and skills, and when you finally place the child, you say, "It is over to you, Lord, I have done all I can."' I found this helpful and often remembered it.

The next chapter is about situations at home, at work, and in the Church in which some women find it difficult to be assertive.

Chapter 7

— *Being More Confident* —

At home

> In a word, accept one another as Christ accepted us,
> to the glory of God.
>
> Romans 15.7

Assertiveness skills are especially useful in our closest family relationships, with parents, partners, children and in-laws. No two relationships are exactly alike. We bring our individual temperaments, social backgrounds, childhood experiences and role models to the relationship, as the other person does. But there are some very general guidelines for using assertive skills in relating to those to whom we feel closest which may be useful.

Being a parent

How we feel about ourselves and the way we relate to others depends in part on our early childhood experiences, on how much love, approval and encouragement we received. But there is no such thing as a perfect childhood or perfect parents. We all experience various degrees of hurt and damage along the way and have to come to terms with this. Easy though it may be to blame our parents, it is not really helpful. It may be better to find out all we can about our parents' childhoods, as the traumas they went through and the affection and security they lacked, may be a guide to what happened to us.

It is well known that family patterns often repeat themselves; physical abuse, for example, may be passed down the generations. But this does not necessarily happen. Some parents are determined not to treat their children as they were treated.

Letting go

It is often said that the art of being a good mother is knowing when to let go. This letting go seems to be a continuous process, starting with letting other people care for your precious baby sometimes and trusting grandparents and friends with older children for longer periods. It is so easy to become possessive.

Some mothers find it very difficult to let go of their adult children. They may have unrealized ambitions and hopes for them and find it difficult to accept them as they are. Many women, although living independently, perhaps with families of their own, are still dependent on their mother's approval to maintain their self-esteem. This may leave them open to manipulation and their mother's dependence on them. Single women may be especially vulnerable to this and many have spent their whole adult lives caring for a parent. Emotional independence is not easy to achieve, especially if their childhood dependence was interrupted or denied.

In our relationships with our parents, children and husbands, the crucial thing to get right is the emotional space between us and them. The amount of space we need varies between individuals and also depends on the stage of our lives we are at. It varies from the intense closeness of a mother and a newborn baby, who still feel 'one flesh', to complete separation.

For some women, the dependency of others is the principal basis of their self-esteem. This may make it particularly difficult for them to let their children go, grow up and be independent. We all want to be loved and needed, but while in some women the maternal, nurturing instinct is dominant, in others it is

55

less strong. (Perhaps this is why pets are such an important part of some people's lives.)

Many of the problems of parenting are connected with the self-esteem of the parents. It is that which determines the amount of space they can give their children. Parents who lack self-confidence may be rigid disciplinarians, not able to be flexible, and threatened by their children's defiance or rudeness. They may also be over-dependent on the love and approval of their children, or over-anxious about their safety, continually watching them and telling them to be careful.

Lone mothers

Lone mothers may be especially vulnerable to low self-esteem and are often made to feel that they are responsible for all the ills of society. Some lone mothers have been left by their partners and some have left home after being abused. Becoming a lone parent may not have been their choice. The majority of them are poor and have a continuous struggle with responsibility and overwork.

Parents with a good sense of their own worth can cope more equably with the range of their children's behaviour, can listen to them, encourage them and be calmly firm when necessary. It is easy to feel we are in competition with other parents, but we all do the best we can, given our specific circumstances and upbringing. Everyone needs support. None of us are perfect parents; we all make lots of mistakes. Understanding the effect on us of our own childhood can help us not to repeat our parents' shortcomings or to over-react in the opposite way.

We know that children want and need to be loved and valued as individuals, that they need physical comfort, cuddling and reassurance. They need to be told we love them, constantly and for ever, and praised for what they do well, for trying or for controlling their jealousy or aggression. Praise is much more effective than blame. It is best to ignore most of their bad behaviour and pay them more attention when they behave well.

The only way to change anyone else's behaviour is to change our reaction to it. When I worked in a child guidance clinic, we used to encourage parents to alter the way they reacted to their child's difficult behaviour. This often worked. Children of all ages need to have boundaries if they are to feel secure. Testing the boundaries is part of growing up. If you are assertive and confident as a parent, your children know where they are with you, what they may do and what they may not. This makes them more secure and so more co-operative.

Apologizing to our children when we have been unjust or irritable or have lost our temper sets an example for them. They need to learn that sometimes we are tired, do not feel well, are stressed or rushed and these are not the best times to ask for things, but, at others, we are relaxed, ready to have fun and play with them and likely to be more lenient. If we try to understand their moods, their tiredness, jealousy, rages and tiresome nagging and make allowances, it can work both ways. You need space and privacy to cope with your own problems and sadness and so do they. (I remember how much I wanted a room of my own as a child, so that I could cry without any-one knowing, but also half wanting someone to come in and comfort me!)

Caring for our parents

As we get older, we may have to cope with the increasing dependency of our own mothers or fathers. This problem was frequently raised on confidence courses that I have run. How we deal with it depends on our complicated and long-standing relationship with our parents and on how dependent we are on their good opinion.

Mothers particularly are sometimes very skilled at manipulating their daughters, making them feel guilty and ungrateful.

They may make quite unreasonable demands. As people are now living longer, an increasing number of women spend all their time caring for their parents. A few may enjoy this role reversal; others feel angry and resentful, but see no alternative. Assertive skills are valuable here. If we can come to terms with the guilt, we can try to limit our involvement to what feels comfortable for us and insist on getting more help if it is necessary. It can be an extremely difficult and painful situation and there are no easy answers.

Husbands or partners

In marriage, the degree of closeness with which we feel comfortable is what is important. When we are first married, we may feel we want complete intimacy, with no secrets and no confidence left unshared. As the years go on, we perhaps recognize that we need space of our own, some private thoughts, friends and activities we may not want to share. It is the freedom and privacy that we allow each other which enables both partners to grow.

As Kahlil Gibran writes in *The Prophet*:

But let there be spaces in your togetherness,
And let the winds of the heavens dance between you . . . .
Sing and dance together and be joyous, but let each one of
  you be alone,
Even as the strings of a lute are alone though they quiver
  with the same music . . . .
Stand together yet not too near together:
For the pillars of the temple stand apart,
And the oak tree and cypress grow not in each other's
  shadow.

Good self-esteem enables us to have loving, honest marriages or partnerships which help us acknowledge our differences (heatedly sometimes) while respecting each other. When my husband was a marriage guidance counsellor he used to say that uneven marriages, where one partner was dominant and the other had low self-esteem, caused problems. I have observed the same. There may also be difficulties if one partner matures faster than the other and changes so much that they are no longer the same person they were when first married. This sometimes happens, for example, if a woman undertakes a further education course, or if a man is promoted to responsible, challenging work which changes him. Both partners need to help each other to mature and grow by encouraging each other to widen their horizons and give greater priority to their own needs.

Talk to each other

Good communication seems to be one of the keys to successful relationships. It is easy to neglect this in a busy life, full of pressures on time and energy. Talking to each other, beyond making practical arrangements, may have to be planned and put in your diaries, a regular slot made for it.

Of course, all marriages, all relationships, are different and there are no easy answers to these problems. But greater confidence, in both partners, does enable each of them to do their share of decision-making, to take more control of their lives. When we are happy, with our basic needs met, we can all be more generous and tolerant; we can say what we want and negotiate. Men and women with low self-esteem and poor assertiveness skills are more likely to manipulate or be aggressive.

Today, some men feel that their role has been changed. Different, confusing demands are made on them, they may no longer be the only or principal bread-winner (or a bread-winner at all) and they are expected to take on more responsibility in the house and with the children. The old balance has been disturbed. Some men seem to enjoy their new roles, but others feel disorientated and may need help and support to adapt.

Men and emotion

Many men are not good at expressing a range of emotion. They recognize anger, but sometimes cannot articulate their jealousy, loneliness, disappointment, hurt or sadness. These feelings are not always part of their vocabulary and they do not know how to express them. They also may be unable to deal with tension at work, be afraid of losing their job, and so take that tension home. They may see asking for any kind of help as unmanly and demeaning.

We women, on the other hand, are taught early in our lives that in order to fulfil our role of nurturer and care-giver we must always put others ahead of ourselves. Rather than be as caring, concerned and protective of ourselves as of others, we may resort to helplessness, which further diminishes our self-esteem. We may also have strongly held beliefs about traditional gender roles in marriage and be confused by new attitudes and expectations.

Divorce

Sadly, however hard we try and however assertive we are, some marriages end in divorce. Abuse, infidelity, incompatibility may be contributing factors. Whatever the reason a marriage breaks up, the pain, anger and sense of failure can be overwhelming. Loving support and, perhaps, practical help may be badly needed. We all make mistakes, and for all sorts of reasons we may not marry the right man. Fortunately many second marriages are happy and long lasting.

Unfortunately, many of the churches, usually so skilled and caring when helping with bereavement, seem unable to cope with this more complex kind of loss. Rather than show the love and forgiveness of the gospels, some churches at best turn their back, not wanting to know, and, at worst, are judgemental and condemning, increasing the existing pain and guilt. The attitudes of some clergy to remarriage in church, and even to admission to communion, cause such anguish that many divorcees leave the church.

Forty years ago, when ill in hospital and expecting my first child, I was refused communion by the hospital chaplain when I told him that my husband had been married previously. This was a devastating rejection for me and took many years to heal. If this happened to me today I should realize that it was just one bigoted man and not God who was rejecting me.

Domestic violence

Communities do not want to acknowledge that domestic violence happens in at least five of every hundred marriages in Britain (Hague and Malos, 1993). We all collude in keeping this secret. This makes it difficult for women who are suffering physical or verbal abuse from their husbands to admit it or to seek help.

When a woman has been abused, she does not expect to be believed. She is ashamed and embarrassed; she expects to be blamed, and often is. At first she may deny the violence even to herself: 'It's not so bad.' She believes that she is responsible, feels guilty and so tries harder to please.

Even when the violence persists, a woman is often reluctant to tell anyone, because of her sense of shame and failure. If her attempts to control or escape the abuse are unsuccessful, her feeling of powerlessness increases and she may sink into a state of chronic despair.

What can we do to prevent becoming the victims of domestic abuse? If we are starting a new relationship or marriage, we should be very firm and assertive at the first sign of physical or verbal abuse, making it clear that we are not prepared to put up with it. If it happens again, we should leave, at least for a while. The man may express regret and a 'honeymoon period' is not uncommon, but he is likely to resort to violence again unless he receives skilled counselling.

If you are being abused, you should get help, advice and support from Women's Aid (look for their phone number in your local phone book, or ask at your Citizens Advice Bureau or the town hall), the Samaritans or, if necessary, the police. You do not have to tolerate abuse and should not believe the names your partner calls you. It is not your fault. We all make mistakes or are incompetent sometimes, but that does not justify violence. Nothing you do can justify your being abused.

Keeping a family together at any price is not safe, nor is it in the best interests of your children. It is not kind or loving to allow a man to continue using violence, whatever the circumstances. He has broken the contract of marriage and you are not bound by any vows to stay with him. It cannot be God's will. Use assertiveness.

Women's Aid have a limited number of refuges and will also help with applications to Social Security and Housing. Some refuges also offer counselling and group support as well, but they do not work in all areas of the country and do not yet have enough places to meet the needs of abused women.

Middle-class women may find it even more difficult to ask for help and we need to be alert to the possibility of abuse in all families known to us. To bring the subject more into the open, it would help if church groups for women invited speakers from Women's Aid to give a talk. This might encourage more women to seek help and also prompt churches to give clearer messages about the unacceptability, the sin, of domestic abuse.

There is a great discrepancy between the justice and love the gospel proclaims and the way the churches are perceived by those who work with the victims of domestic violence. If the churches were more outspoken, stating unequivocably that violence is wrong, whatever the provocation, and that there are better ways to resolve problems, they would be a positive influence in this area.

Assertiveness at work

Many women find it difficult to behave assertively at work. Sometimes this is because they are in a junior position and have so little authority that it is 'not their place' to change anything. But it may be because they are afraid of what others think, afraid that they may get a reputation for being awkward or touchy, which might interfere with their job security or chances of promotion. In most jobs, if we are to progress, we need to be seen as strong, positive, enthusiastic and willing to take responsibility. So assertiveness, not aggression, can often be the way to improve conditions, change attitudes at work and obtain promotion.

Discrimination

You have a right to equal opportunities. Exercise it.
Equal Opportunities Commission

It is unlawful to treat anyone, on the grounds of their sex, less favourably than a person of the opposite sex would be treated in the same circumstances. Sex discrimination is not allowed in employment, education, housing, facilities or advertising. In employment it is also unlawful to discriminate because a person is married. Women are entitled, under the Equal Pay Act 1970, to equal pay with men when doing the same work and it is worth keeping a check on this.

In recent times it is an indirect form of discrimination which most women experience. When considering appointments, preference is often given to those with an unbroken work record, a willingness to work long hours, mobility and educational achievements. This can work against you if you have children or give some priority to your family life and it is hard to prove sex discrimination in such situations.

Whether you work in an environment that is largely female

or one where women are in a minority, you may face subtle discrimination, or blatant sexism, from colleagues or from the organization. Both are difficult to challenge, because the spotlight tends to fall on your behaviour. If you complain, they may say 'She can't take a joke' or 'She's a whingeing feminist.'

Joan works in the meat room in a major branch of a national food retailer. The qualified butchers are all men, as are the other meat-room staff. At one time Joan had a woman colleague, but she moved to another department. Together the two women had been able to counteract some of the 'laddishness' of their male colleagues and had been a support to each other, but on her own Joan found the working atmosphere increasingly difficult. The nature of the conversations not only excluded her but made her feel extremely uncomfortable. She began to dread going to work. Joan, who appears to be a fairly mild person, eventually decided that she could put up with things no longer. She did not ask to be transferred but instead, the next time the conversation started to become offensive, she objected in no uncertain terms. As she put it, she 'really had a go at them' and then she spoke firmly to her male manager. Things immediately improved but, if they deteriorate, Joan is ready to speak out again.

Women as sex objects

Challenging blatant behaviour like this may seem easier than tackling subtle sexism, but it still needs a great deal of courage, especially if you are suffering from low self-esteem. It is important to remember that discrimination and harassment are not your fault. Some men have been conditioned to treat women as inferior or as sex objects. We have to teach them new ways of relating and make sure our sons grow up treating women as people. I believe that this can only happen if we improve our own self-esteem and learn to be more assertive.

Increasingly, work-places are establishing policies on sexual harassment, so a first step is to be familiar with the policy and how to use it. If your place of work does not have a policy, perhaps you could suggest to staff representatives that one should be developed. You do not have to deal with sexual harassment on your own. Trades union representatives or personnel officers will support you in tackling it and, if necessary, help put together the evidence needed to take disciplinary action against the offender. Harassment can include innuendoes and personal remarks as well as fondling, bottom-pinching and more serious physical abuse. Complaints of this kind are often kept on file and, in a recent case in the Fire Service, a senior officer was dismissed after four women had made separate complaints about his behaviour.

Gender bias has existed for many centuries and affects our closest relationships. It is enshrined in our culture and the force of law cannot change it overnight, so we must find the courage to challenge it whenever we can. Perhaps we can start by persuading the men we are close to to be more sensitive about making personal remarks about women's size, sexiness or body parts. Even if they are made in a good-humoured or complimentary way, remarks of this kind may not be acceptable, especially at work. A man should be sure that the woman is really comfortable with this kind of approach before he pursues it. If we are to change the 'laddish' culture prevalent in some parts of our society, we must respond assertively, as Joan did, and enlist the help of men in changing this ethos. How *you* react to these kinds of remark will either help men change or confirm them in the behaviour.

Racism

Discrimination on grounds of race is, of course, also against the law. On the whole, Christians accept that racism is not acceptable, but there is still a great deal of prejudice in all areas. Black women suffer from a double discrimination and may have to be very assertive to overcome it. Like everyone else, they fail sometimes, but their mistakes may be put down to their colour and held against them.

> You are at an office meeting and someone makes racist remarks about a new Asian member of staff who is not present. Do you:
>
> • smile and say nothing?
> • look disapproving and say nothing?
> • gently but firmly say that the remark is racist and you do not agree with it?
>
> The last alternative may be helpful, but what is really needed is support and friendship for her/him in the office. It is not an easy situation. However, if you say nothing, you are colluding and encouraging racism.

It is not always possible to pick up on every piece of discriminatory behaviour at work, but it is possible, little by little, to make people more aware of their behaviour and so give them the option to change. Like gender bias, much racism is unconscious and we all need to be conscious of the remnants of it in ourselves.

Women as managers and leaders

Women often underestimate their abilities and do not put themselves forward for senior positions without considerable encouragement. This may be because of low self-esteem, some causes of which we have already examined. It may be because they do not want to be in charge of men or because the structure of the organization is uncongenial. They may not want extra responsibility or to be seen as pushing themselves forward (pushy women are seen as unfeminine). It may also be that they are reluctant to face the amount of indirect discrimination and verbal abuse directed at women who apply for senior positions in some fields.

Women leaders often have a lot of pressure put on them, much more than on men, and need a great deal of support from other women. Those with children or elderly relatives have to deal with the problem of juggling care arrangements and the guilt and conflict involved in having dual roles. However, many women do manage this successfully.

Some women choose to be leaders in the style of men, concerned with hierarchy and authority, as this has been the style of their previous bosses and what seems to be expected. If you have been lucky enough to have had women managers who were supportive and prepared to share responsibility, but also encouraged initiative and new ideas, as I have, you can use them as role models. Of course, men can be collaborative and supportive, too, but some are more hierarchical and ambitious and resent the changes they may have to make if they are to work with women as colleagues.

If you are in a position of responsibility at work, you may find these 'basics of team leadership' helpful:

- Treat all employees equally and give each personal attention as required.
- Keep the promises you make to all team members.
- Be consistent and act positively, even if you feel negative.
- Set a good example on appearance, punctuality and time-keeping and support company policies and procedures.
- Stay calm under pressure. Others tend to imitate a leader's reactions.
- Provide regular opportunities to meet and exchange ideas with team members.
- Make sure goals are clearly communicated and understood.
- Listen to other people's ideas and, when possible, act on them.
- Make decisions firmly, even if they upset some people.

Chapter 8

── *Speaking Up in Church* ──

For freedom Christ has set us free. Stand firm, therefore, and do not submit again to a yoke of slavery.

Galatians 15.1

What a challenge this is to stand up for what we believe is
right. The church we go to may be a comfortable place for us
and we may not want anything to change. We may think that
behaving assertively in a church situation would be out of the
question. We have been taught as children that we must be on
our best behaviour in church. This means being quiet and
'good'. No wonder it is so hard to make changes!

Direct discrimination

Only religious institutions are allowed by law to discriminate
directly against women. After a long and painful campaign to
persuade the Church of England to admit women to the priest-
hood, their ordination was agreed by the General Synod on 11
November 1992. But, because some clergy and lay people had
such strong objections 'on principle', individual parishes are
permitted to refuse ministry from a woman priest or from a
bishop who ordains women. This perpetuates direct discrimination in some places and gives women a very mixed message.

There are now women clergy in all but the Roman Catholic

and Orthodox churches. The Methodists have ordained women since 1974, the Congregational Church (now part of the United Reformed Church) and the Baptists since 1917. In most churches, lay women can now read lessons, preach, administer the chalice and sit on church councils and synods. Despite this progress, many hurtful statements deriding women have been made, even in our lifetime, which must affect our self-confidence.

Changing the Church, meaning all the Christian churches, involves more than changing the rules about women ministers. It involves changing basic attitudes of both men and women to allow the talents of each to be used to the full.

The example of Jesus

Jesus's attitude to women broke the cultural taboos of the time. He talked to women alone, even 'unclean' foreign women (John 4.7–27), listened to them, taught them, allowed them to touch him (Mark 5.25–34), touched, healed and valued them and let them travel with the inner circle of his disciples (Luke 8.1–3). His attitude contrasted with that of most of his contemporaries. There is evidence that, encouraged by the new status and self-esteem Jesus had given them, women played an important part in the early Church, acting as church leaders (Romans 16.1–7). In Galatians 3.28–9 St Paul writes: 'There is no such thing as Jew and Greek, slave and freeman, male and female; for you are all one in Christ Jesus.'

The gospel taught a radical equality between men and women but, as the Church developed, the attitude to women changed, so that they were given more subservient roles, were not allowed to handle holy things and were excluded from the sanctuary. The message was that women were inferior and, when menstruating or pregnant, unclean. Authority and power in the Church was largely exercised by men, with a few notable, and often saintly, exceptions such as St Teresa of Avila and St

Hilda of Whitby, who had a great deal of power and influence and were not limited by lack of self-esteem.

Indirect discrimination

Sadly, there is still indirect discrimination from some clergy, church officials and laity (men and women) in all the churches, even among those who do not object to the principle of women priests. Some of it is unconscious, the result of habit and conditioning, and some is more deliberate. Senior male clergy who make patronizing remarks to women may not intend to be offensive. If they are not aware of what effect they have, who is to tell them? How will they learn?

> A woman priest apologized to the male chairman for being unable to attend the next committee meeting. He replied, 'That's all right. I never notice whether you are there or not!' Unfortunately, she did not reply. She was angry and hurt but 'did not like to say anything'.

> A male colleague said to another woman priest, 'Whenever I think of you, I wonder what you are like in bed.' The woman replied, 'That's funny. Whenever I think of you, I never wonder what you are like in bed!'

As long as women tell stories about themselves as the victims of men's insensitivity, but do nothing about responding more assertively, as in the first of these examples, the injustice will continue. If we can stop worrying about being seen as 'good girls', wanting to be feminine and attractive to men, we can risk responding to sexist remarks in the way they deserve, as the second story illustrates. These true stories are common. You may have experienced something similar yourself and know how hurtful it can be. Incidents such as these may seem trivial, but, constantly repeated, they become a huge burden on women priests and other women. They damage their self-esteem and limit the effective use of their gifts.

We have been so conditioned to be polite and respectful to men, especially clergy, that it is very difficult for us to act assertively. We may criticize them to our friends, we may even leave the church, but to answer directly and honestly is often more than we can manage. Like some laymen, some male clergy can be arrogant and patronizing, but many are sympathetic and try hard not to be sexist. These same men can also seem astonishingly vulnerable, overworked and stressed. We want to be helpful, to be friends with them. They may bring out our maternal, caring and supportive side, making it even more difficult to stand up to them or say no. Some clergy undoubtedly exploit this, enjoying a cosy, helpful and admiring inner circle, perhaps known locally as 'the vicar's fan club'. An élite or inner circle may be useful, but will tend to exclude any who criticize, however constructively.

Women clergy may be shown off as the 'pet', regarded as the fearsome nanny figure ('We're all terrified of her') or treated as a comfortable mother figure and put to work with children and the elderly. Women clergy have found it difficult to be accepted in some parishes and districts and many work as hospital and school chaplains or in training posts. Wherever they work, they need the support and encouragement of other women as they pioneer a new kind of ministry in the face of many difficulties.

Exclusive language

The minister preached about how we are all 'brothers of Christ', repeating the phrase again and again without qualification. Jane felt hurt and totally excluded from the rest of the service. She managed to wait until the rest of the congregation had left and then told the minister how excluded she had felt. She could not be anyone's 'brother'. To do the minister credit, he was very apologetic and humbly promised to try to be more sensitive in his use of language in the future.

71

If Jane had not decided to speak to him at the first opportunity:

- She would have continued to feel hurt and angry.
- She might have internalized her sense of rejection and believed that only men could have a close relationship with Christ, that she, as a woman, was in some way inferior, unworthy. (That is, after all, what women have been taught for centuries.)
- She might have walked out of the service.
- She might have stopped going to church.
- She might have complained to her friends and got their support.

Which of these would be your reaction?
Which would be best for your self-esteem and mental health?
Which would be best for the Church?

It seems that many people are drawn to the Church because they dislike and fear change and want to find a refuge where everything remains the same. This conservatism may be part of their personality or may be due to insecurity caused by past experiences. This insecurity should be respected. We too may be insecure, but if we are to widen our horizons we shall need to be more adventurous and prepared to try what we have never tried before.

Inclusive language

The subject of inclusive language arouses strong feelings and understandable objections, on aesthetic and nostalgic grounds. We may have grown up with the beautiful old language, and love it. This nostalgia becomes a reason in itself for keeping the liturgy, or words of the services, intact. Until recently, the language of church services was not questioned, and when we were quite young we learned to know when 'men' meant us too and when it did not. Changing 'men' to 'men and women' or 'people' in the words of services is surely possible? The poetry of some of the hymns may be too beautiful to alter, but with others a simple change or omission would make those women who are now aware feel more included. This already happens in many churches.

For example, why not change 'he' to 'she' in Bunyan's hymn 'Who would true valour see' if most of the congregation are women? In the last verse, some versions change 'he' to 'we' and 'I', and substitute 'they' for 'men', as in: 'I'll fear not what they say, I'll labour night and day, to be a pilgrim.'

Changing structures

The women members of churches do much of the maintenance work, cleaning, organizing, feeding people and working with women's church organizations. We arrange flowers, raise money, staff church bazaars, visit the sick and work with children. In recent years, more women have served on church councils and committees, and as wardens and elders, but we are still in a minority. Even when we find the confidence to take on these responsible tasks, we still have to find the courage to speak and to put forward what may be a very different point of view. We may be listened to regarding pastoral matters or catering arrangements, for example, but less often when it comes to decisions to do with buildings or finance.

I believe that a church which is less authoritarian and hier-archical, and more interactive, encouraging consultation and co-operation, would attract more people and do more to encourage the spiritual growth of individuals. It might seem relevant to more people if the liturgy, or forms of service, were more flexible, if there was greater use of the words of women and men of God through the ages, as well as the Bible, and less stress on the history of the Church and more on Christ's presence with us today.

We all have different priorities and there is room for variety.

I would like to see a change in the Church's priorities, to address the issues of poverty, justice and abuse with more urgency. We women need to make our voices heard. We need to learn about the existing organization of our churches. We need to learn to read balance sheets and to understand accounts. Most importantly, we must learn to put our point of view assertively, not aggressively, recruiting the support of other women and men.

There is nothing easy or comfortable about questioning embedded patterns of behaviour and deeply cherished beliefs. Challenging tradition can be difficult and uncomfortable, even in groups which might be expected to be aware of the issues.

A laywoman, Laura, was at a meeting of church workers, including six male clergy and one other laywoman. The group had worked together for some time and knew each other quite well. One of the clergymen described a meeting he had had with an American woman who was offering to assist with a particular piece of work. His description included the woman's age, height and dress. Laura felt that these things would not have been included in a description of a meeting with a man. The clergyman had clearly felt unnerved by the strong American woman. If she had been a man, she would almost certainly have been described as charismatic or energetic, rather than in physical terms. Laura decided to challenge the description but, as she did so, she was aware of her own anxiety and the fear that she might be seen as criticizing a colleague. Her comments were accepted, but throughout the rest of the meeting the group referred to them in a joky manner, to hide their embarrassment, perhaps.

How to get things changed

If you want to change attitudes in your church, school or wider community, perhaps you should take on more responsibility.

Would you like to be on a church, parish or district council? Or stand for office? Perhaps you are already on such a committee. Do you have the courage to speak?

- Attend meetings as an observer, and go to the AGM.
- Tell your vicar/minister/the chairperson that you are interested.
- Be clear about what you can contribute; know your strengths.
- Ask for explanations or more information where necessary. (You may not be the only one who does not understand the jargon or use of initials!)
- Get to know someone on the committee and ask them to explain its history and who is who.
- Make allies on the committee, lobby them and get them to support you.
- If you feel something instinctively, it is worth saying so: others may feel the same and it can then be discussed.
- Speak for the timid women, the voiceless, the excluded.
- Get information. Use books, leaflets, newspapers and organizations.
- Ask someone to teach you to read a balance sheet, if you do not already know.
- Say what you think assertively, without aggression or apology. You have a right to your opinion. (Your colleagues have a right to disagree!)
- Be very clear about how much time you can offer and what interests you. You may be much in demand.

I find it difficult to understand women and men who turn up faithfully to church meetings and then say nothing. What are their ideas and their opinions? Sometimes they will give their views if asked directly by the chair. We should try to help them have more confidence in their own value and their own views.

When I was first asked to chair the Oxford diocese's committee for the Ecumenical Decade of Churches in

Solidarity with Women, I found it very difficult. Although I had chaired many meetings as a social worker, this seemed quite different. I was not familiar with the structure, the jargon or, above all, the use of initials for organizations and departments. I felt very stupid, either struggling to decipher what they meant, or having to ask about things everyone else knew. Eventually I got used to the job and really enjoyed it. This book is a result!

Social situations

On the confidence courses we have run, the subject of coffee after church is frequently discussed. This is always viewed as a difficult time. It is not making the drinks or passing them round that is difficult, but standing around wondering if anyone could possibly want to talk to you. If this is awkward and embarrassing for regular church-goers, who presumably have friends and acquaintances in the congregation, how much more difficult it must be for newcomers. Perhaps the least confident just scuttle out of the door murmuring 'Must put the lunch on' or 'I've got guests coming.' How do you cope? Do you join the scuttlers? I have been known to!

Jill, a rather shy friend of mine, told me that she says: 'Lord, who do you want me to talk to?' Then she does as she is told! Another possibility is to find someone who looks even more shy and awkward than you feel and see how quickly you can make them relax. Asking fairly general questions may be a good starter. A tip I learned recently is to think of conversation as a game of catch. You bounce the ball back and forth between you, not keeping it too long or allowing the other to hold it indefinitely.

Another difficulty some people mention concerns sharing the peace. When the practice was first introduced in our church, one warden was appalled at the idea of 'shaking hands with someone you have not been introduced to'. I have also been told of men who exploit the peace and insist on kissing or even hugging women inappropriately. Many women use the firm, stiff-arm handshake to ward off embraces which are not welcome, while others suffer them in silence. I am sure that in many churches sharing the peace is a warm, friendly part of the service which makes people feel more included and welcome, but to kiss women who do not wish to be kissed is a form of assault.

If these situations seem unproblematic and trivial to you, I assure you that they are not to everyone. To women already suffering from low self-esteem they may be major hurdles.

An American woman who had been on a confidence course wrote:

As a result of the course I was able to confront the issue of prejudice on a church training course which I am involved in. First I was able to go to the lecturer and explain why I believed negative comments on my country's decisions on social issues were being framed in a prejudicial manner. Then I was able to confront a fellow student who frequently made prejudiced remarks in the class situation. Through that verbal exchange, which was quite intense, I was able to stay (relatively) calm and coherent (very). It took two more discussions before the issue was resolved, the person involved finally 'heard' what I was saying and peace was restored. In these discussions I was able to be compassionate, but clear and firm, staying with the issue and not being side-tracked into being 'nice' and apologetic to this man.

Discovering talent (or finding gold)

The account in St John's Gospel of the feeding of the five thousand includes Jesus saying: 'Gather up the fragments left over, so that nothing may be lost' (6.13). Did he mean just the

77

crumbs from the loaves and fishes? Or did he mean that we should not waste our gifts and talents?

If the church is 'the body of Christ', it must surely include and welcome everyone, those on the fringes as well as the select band who attend and help regularly. We often use the same people again and again until they are exhausted. They seem to be reliable and willing, but we may be excluding others whose talents go untapped.

Hilda had studied art before her marriage. With little confidence in herself or her own abilities, her life was subordinated to that of her talented husband, who excelled in his professional life and as a musician. She joined a supportive women's church group and was persuaded to share some of her work with them. Over the next eight years she became the person the church turned to for any design or artistic work. She helped the children make collages at Christmas, produced programmes and posters and displayed her paintings at a local exhibition.

If you are an organizer, perhaps in your church or community, why not ask some of the less outgoing, less obviously capable members to help? And not just to clean or arrange flowers, though that may be a start. Work on the assumption that people are like icebergs: most of their gifts lie unused, hidden beneath the surface. If we can help these gifts to be realized, instead of wasted, we can enrich that individual, and help raise their self-esteem.

My grandfather was an engineer and prospected for gold in northern Canada. Perhaps because of this, I particularly like the expression and idea of 'there is gold in everyone', meaning talent and goodness and potential. I believe we need to prospect both for the gold in ourselves and the gold in others. Sometimes the gold is obvious, lying on the surface, as it were, but sometimes it is necessary to

78

mine for it, to dig deep beneath outward appearances, layers of habit and apathy, to find it. It is in everyone. Another way to put it is to call it 'the light of Christ'. If we can believe in it ourselves and in others, we can find it, however long it takes, however painful the mining.

As a social worker, I have known depressed and needy people, often with very little confidence in themselves, transformed by even the suggestion that they could help others. We ourselves know that nothing improves our morale more, and snaps us out of feeling sorry for ourselves, than feeling that we are needed. One way of helping may be to suggest that people with particular needs, such as having a child with a disability, might offer their help to someone in a similar situation, or at a day centre, school or nursery. Communities need not be divided into those who need help and those who can give it. We all need help at some time and we can all give it. What we need are more miners!

A client, Karen, who was in the early stages of multiple sclerosis, had become so depressed that she did not use the abilities she had and was extremely disagreeable to her family. Counselling did not seem to help. One day I mentioned that voluntary help was needed at the day centre for the elderly. She brightened immediately and for three weeks went regularly, twice a week, to read out bingo numbers. But the day centre found her bad language a liability and asked me to stop her going. Rather dreading this task, I called to see her. She met me with: 'That job you got me, they didn't pay me. I've got a job at the launderette instead.' Karen did not look back. Her confidence was restored and she forgot about being an invalid.

I remember once persuading two lonely house-bound old men that they should phone each other every day for a chat. I promised to find some help with their phone bills. Six weeks later they phoned to say they had discovered they were both interested in horse-racing and had made a lot of money on their bets, so not to worry about help with the bills. They never met, but their lives were enriched in more ways than one!

If we are really concerned about others in the community, or in our own families, we need to use our brains and imaginations as well as our tender hearts. We tend to think only of offering ourselves, our sympathy and care, and that there are people who need us and what we alone can give. But we have to accept that there are some people we are not able to help, perhaps because we are not qualified or experienced enough to deal with their deep traumas. It may be that the person we are trying to help needs encouragement to seek professional assistance, a marriage guidance counsellor or psychologist, for example.

There are suggestions about voluntary work in Appendix 2.

Chapter 9

— New Life Within Us —

To another he said, 'Follow me.' But he said, 'Lord, first let me go and bury my father.' But Jesus said to him, 'Let the dead bury their own dead; but as for you, go and proclaim the kingdom of God.' Another said, 'I will follow you, Lord, but let me first say farewell to those at my home.' Jesus said to him, 'No one who puts a hand to the plough and looks back is fit for the kingdom of God.'

Luke 9.59–62

After this he went out and saw a tax collector named Levi sitting at the tax booth; and he said to him, 'Follow me.' And he got up and left everything and followed him.

Luke 5.27

Vocation

Of these two reactions to Jesus's call to follow him, the first seems more understandable and Jesus's response rather harsh.

How do we know what God intends for us? What does 'Follow me' mean for us? We may have vague longings, that will not be silenced, to do or be something else. This may be God nudging us in a new direction. We may have to struggle to translate these vague longings into the discovery of our vocation. This may mean taking on a new role, perhaps training for a new job, or some part-time voluntary work. Or it may be that we continue what we are doing, but with new heart. It will involve using the gifts that are special and unique to us in order that we may become a gift to others.

Assertiveness skills are not usually thought of as applying to our spiritual lives, but I suggest they could be. If we really believe that God put us on this earth for a purpose and has special work for us to do, that must give us the confidence, first to discover what our vocation is (if we do not know already) and then to have the strength and determination to live it. It may take a great deal of effort and all our skills to do what we believe is God's will. The first hurdle may be our own apathy or lack of confidence in our vocation.

> One afternoon many years ago, when I worked for Social Services, I was told that I had not got the promotion I expected. I felt hurt and very angry, almost speechless with rage. I went to my car, cried and raged for some time, then remembered that I had promised to visit a family. Soon after I arrived, the 14-year-old daughter, Linda, came home, shouted at her mother and ran, weeping, upstairs. I went up. Linda was in her chaotic, curtainless bedroom, which was bare except for a sagging iron bedstead and mattress. I sat on the uncomfortable bed and listened to her. I must have really listened, as I can still remember what she said. As she talked, I had an amazing experience. I became certain, quite positive, that sitting on that bed, listening to Linda, was exactly what God wanted me to do. I was where he wanted me to be, even though there was little I could do to help her. My hurt, anger and dis-appointment about not getting promotion vanished. Next day at work my colleagues were astonished at the overnight transformation in me and my acceptance of the decision.

To discover our true vocation we need to explore those things that we already know. It is worth while to look at what we have always dreamed about doing. If you could do anything, what would you really like to do? My experience of asking many people that question, is that our dreams are rarely impossible, often only one step away from where we are. One woman told me she had always wanted to go up in a glider. This proved impossible for medical reasons, so she went up in a balloon instead! Others have talked about getting a poem published, or going to India. The mother of a severely disabled child longed to go to the circus. It took two years of gradually separating from her child, enough to leave her in her father's care for an evening. She eventually went to the circus. It represented a major change in her life.

Dreams like this, that at first seem trivial, may be a clue to something significant. Is it possible that our dreams are God-given? Are they so impossible? If we can pursue the things that make our hearts sing, we will be doing what God wants us to do and discover our true vocation. We need to learn to trust our hunches, our dreams, as they may be right. Get advice and information, if you need to, but be prepared to take risks and do a lot of hard work.

> Sara, a friend of mine, dreamed of working in films. She was divorced, with three children, and had no academic qualifications at all. She started an Open University course in sociology, but was then accepted for a four-year course at a local university. With support from her friends, she worked hard and got a good degree. She now has a job in television and has grown immeasurably, not only intellectually but in maturity.

New life within us

At the Annunciation, the angel came to tell Mary of the new life hidden within her. What does that mean for us? Can we recognize, accept and give birth to the new life that is God within us? There is in all of us so much hidden life, such richness, so many talents and such potential for love, creativity and holiness. Most of us use only a very small part of the gifts God has given us. If we can open ourselves to accept, nurture and develop that new life and become what God intends, we, our families, the Church and the world will be richer.

As women who have had children know, giving birth is painful, often traumatic, and caring for a new life takes time, effort, patience and much love. It involves major changes in life-style, different priorities, an enlargement of our area of concern. In the same way, new spiritual life can mean a painful period of discovery. New friends may challenge our values. New ideas may conflict with certainties on which we have based our lives. A new commitment to more open, honest relationships will need practice, perseverance and much painful heart-searching.

Most of us live in a small world constricted by duties, by the expectations of others and perhaps by our own resistance to change. But we do have choices. There are many ways of expanding our horizons spiritually. Books – biographies, history, travel, novels, poetry of all kinds and, of course, books on prayer and spirituality – may open windows for some people. Listening to or making music, looking at paintings (or painting yourself) can enlarge the spirit and imagination. Outdoor activities or gardening are important to others. Each of us is unique and different things inspire and excite us.

I like poetry which I do not fully understand and which seems to point towards a holiness and mystery beyond my experience, T. S. Eliot's *Four Quartets*, for example. In his poetry he seems to be describing a mystery that we cannot grasp with our minds but which tugs at our hearts like the pull of gravity.

My favourite is 'Ash Wednesday':

> Blessèd sister, holy mother, spirit of the fountain, spirit
>   of the garden,
> Suffer us not to mock ourselves with falsehood
> Teach us to care and not to care

Teach us to sit still
Even among these rocks,
Our peace in His will
And even among these rocks
Sister, mother
And spirit of the river, spirit of the sea,
Suffer me not to be separated

And let my cry come unto Thee

Finding God

How do we get even a glimpse, a flicker of understanding of this mystery? Where do we find God, feel closer to him? The world is so beautiful, so amazing. God created it for us to enjoy, to care for, and to find him through its beauty. Many people feel closer to God, more fully themselves and more in touch with the mystery in wilderness, in forests, by lakes, by the sea, in a garden or in the mountains. Others feel closer when they are helping those in pain, relieving suffering, or perhaps when they look at the face of a beloved child. We are all different. We need to be reminded both of our smallness and of the greatness of God, but also of our part in this wonderful world. We are not outside observers, but a unique part of God's creation, loved and valued by him. That is the mind-blowing part of it!

If we are open and aware enough, we can be more conscious of God's presence in our everyday lives and respond with prayer. For many people, of all faiths, lighting a candle is a reminder of God's presence. Drawing the curtains on a sunny morning can make us rejoice and give thanks. Hands-on tasks like kneeling to weed the garden or sow seeds, sweeping the floor, kneading dough, picking fruit, lighting fires and collecting wood, which have been done over the centuries by women (and men), seem to connect us with our deepest selves and also with our foremothers, their struggles and search for meaning.

When doing these jobs I like to think of all those, down the centuries, who have done the same things and try to imagine their circumstances. I belong to a small women's prayer group. We are quiet together, silently praying, meditating or just relaxing, but also we paint, model clay, sew, walk or write poetry as part of our meditation.

A friend of mine says that turning on the cold tap is what triggers her awareness of God. For another, plugging in the kettle is like the bell in a monastery, a time to leave what you are doing and pray. Another finds that quietly stroking a cat on her lap brings her more in touch with God's love.

- What helps you to be conscious of being connected?
- What triggers a prayerful response in you?

We may block ourselves off from so much joy, from God, because of our limited vision. Anything may happen if we are open. God is the God of surprises. We must never limit our expectations or our understanding of him by ascribing a form or gender to him. We know that God has no gender and is more than both genders, yet people feel startled and shocked when God is referred to as 'She'.

We are sometimes aware of something so unexpected and wonderful that it is almost frightening. We cannot speak about it because we are afraid of being thought odd, cranky, even mad. In the Bible, God spoke to people, both directly and through angels. When something happens to us, when we hear or see or feel something we cannot account for and cannot describe, we may treasure it or we may deny it. But we can humbly respond to it. Responding to God is continuous: we never arrive at our destination; the mystery is infinite and we can only get glimpses of a tiny part.

My father and godfather both died when I was eight. As a

small child, I used to believe that heaven was in the sky and the stars were chinks of heavenly light, showing through tiny holes in the black ceiling of the world, through which God, and those in heaven with him, watched over us. This sense of being watched over and cared for has remained with me.

In 1947/8 I worked for the National Children's Home as an assistant housemother. Two of us looked after 22 children aged between 2 and 15. We were given tickets to the Royal Tournament and I took seven excited children to London to see it. The climax of the day, and the most eagerly anticipated, was to be tea in a café with fish and chips. Rationing was still severe and the children rarely had the food they liked.

On the way back to King's Cross on the tube after the show, I discovered that I had lost our return train tickets, having probably handed them in with the outward ones. I remember praying hard on the escalator and then breaking it to the children that we would have to buy new tickets. They took it stoically. I felt terrible. We had enough money for a pot of tea and bread and butter. I was just pouring the tea when a woman who had been sitting at the back of the restaurant passed on her way out. She put a pound note beside me, said: 'Please spend this on your children' and went before I could thank her. A pound was exactly enough for eight fish and chips. We had a feast.

On the train home we discussed what had happened. 'Was it a miracle?' the children asked. We decided it was.

The following Sunday, the minister started his sermon with: 'I don't expect any of you have seen a miracle.' Seven hands shot up – 'Please, sir, we have' – and out came the story, in a rather garbled form. The minister coped well; he agreed it was a miracle. It must have ruined his sermon.

I have always wished that I could thank the woman and

tell her how much her generous gesture meant to me and to the children. It was far more than a plate of fish and chips, a real sense of being watched over and prayer being answered.

Prayer and meditation

Listening to God, to the moving of the Spirit, is usually an aspect of prayer, of meditation. This may already be an important part of your life and you may find it easy and natural. If not, there are many books to help you with this (some are listed at the back of this book). If you find meditation difficult, as I do, you could try lying on your back or sitting comfortably, under trees, on a hill, by the sea, in a garden or in your own room, and just listen to the silence.

- Breathe slowly and regularly.
- Try not to fix your wandering thoughts. Simply watch them sailing by as if you were watching boats going down a river.
- Try not to do anything. Just be open, awake and aware.
- Live in the moment; savour the moment.

Archbishop Anthony Bloom once told a woman who said she found prayer difficult to go into her room, close the door and knit before the face of God. I have found that helpful.

In contemplative prayer we seek to become the person we are called to be, not by thinking of God but by being with God. Simply to be with God is to be drawn into being the person God calls us to be.

John Main

Expanding our horizons

Expanding our horizons physically, emotionally and spiritually will provide more opportunities to develop our gifts and discover what God intends us to do and be. Most of us tend to get a bit 'stuck in a rut', limited by our prejudices, by habit and inertia from exploring more of God's wonderful world. There may be many reasons why we do not always follow the promptings of our inner selves and pursue our longings, and why we feel we cannot lead fuller lives. Lack of energy may prevent us trying new things, especially as we get older or if we are not well. We are just too tired when the demands of work, home and family have been met to even try doing anything different. Pressures of time, responsibilities, caring for others, occupy us.

Would we care better, and feel less resentful and constrained, if we gave greater priority to ourselves, as I have suggested in this book? Is it possible to negotiate more time, to give our needs and our gifts more recognition? Getting out of a rut (if we can find the 'oomph') can actually give us more energy and our family and colleagues are bound to benefit.

Allow some space for your own needs and your own growth: if the very idea produces guilt, where does this come from? If God loves and values us so much, should we not value ourselves more?

Small steps

Trying new things can seem risky and it may seem safer and more comfortable to stick with what we know. If you want to change, to expand your horizons, start slowly and gently, taking very small steps at first. Try:

- reading a different newspaper
- experimenting with a new recipe or different food (an exotic fruit from the supermarket)
- wearing a new, bright colour
- asking someone you hardly know to come for coffee
- taking up activities you once enjoyed (painting, singing, needlework)

89

- going somewhere, perhaps quite close by, you have never been before
- going somewhere alone (visit a garden or an art gallery).

Barriers to change

Finding reasons not to change is not difficult. Like the men in the Bible called to follow Jesus (Luke 14.18), we too have land to see to (the lawn to mow) or fathers to bury (or care for) (Luke 9.59–60). There are always good reasons why now is not a good time to answer the call. It is your choice.

Partners

For those who are married, or in long-term relationships, 'the reaction of my husband/partner' is another very common reason for not making any changes. If this is so for you, the process of change will need careful negotiation and tact. If your husband is going to have a 'new' wife, it must happen slowly and gently, and in such a way that he can see benefits for himself as well as for you. Perhaps he would be interested in this new adventure. A number of widows have told me that they only discovered themselves as people, only discovered their gifts and their strengths, after their husbands died. How sad that these gifts did not enrich their marriages and make them more interesting partners.

Poor health or disability

These may limit our opportunities, but we do still have choices. We can change what we choose to read or watch on television, how we listen to others and the way we relate to those who care for us.

While staying in Chicago, I was taken to meet May. She was in her thirties, and paralysed from the neck down. She could hear, speak and move the tips of her fingers.

90

She lay on a narrow bed, raised to make it easier for her to be washed, changed and fed. She was cared for by friends and neighbours, but lived alone in her bungalow. While I talked to her, she was being washed and changed. My embarrassment lasted only a moment, as she took charge of the situation and asked me to describe my garden in England, 'walk her round it'. Whenever we were diverted, she took me back to where we had stopped, remembering every detail. I have never met anyone who gave her attention so completely and was so interested. It was an extraordinary gift.

May had headphones and the numbers at her fingertips. Her job, she explained, was to give 'wake-up calls'. She was paid by the phone company. Her voluntary work was for an organization similar to the Samaritans. People who were desperate phoned, usually in the middle of the night. She described this quite matter-of-factly, 'You see, I can sleep any time.' She gave them her complete attention.

She was a remarkable and inspiring woman who used to the full every part of herself that was still functioning. Her vitality and love shone out so that her wasted body became irrelevant.

Growing older

This may also be used as a reason for not changing, but it can give us new opportunities to dare to be fully ourselves: the child, the adult and the wise woman. If we can contact, love and understand the hurt, bewildered child within us, we will be able to keep our child's sense of fun, our awareness of magic, the sense of awe and excitement of discovery.

The responsible, caring, maternal adult within us may be less active than she was. But the wise old(er) woman acknowledges and develops the skills and wisdom learnt over a lifetime. She can defy the stereotypes of 'an older woman', resist ageist

labels and be 'a sign of contradiction', not necessarily con-
forming to the expectations of society. She can recognize her
courage in facing past pain, loss, failure and countless disap-
pointments, but also her triumphs, her strength and patience.
She can rediscover the idealism of her youth while accepting
that there is no need for perfection, and that making a fool of
herself is not a disaster.

Old age should be valued more. It frees us from competi-
tiveness, sexual jealousy and the need to attract men. We need
not be dependent on the opinions of others, but, valuing our
own uniqueness, can try new ways of living and relating.

Try not to say, or even think, 'I am too old to do that.' Everest
may be out, but not all climbing happens in the mountains. To
inspire and encourage you, get to know strong, energetic and
creative women.

This poem was written as 'homework' for a 'Growing old
disgracefully' course:

My Dreams

Was it only yesterday, those dreams of things to be?
Goals seemed so very reachable, when I was only three.

I knew that I could be a star of stage or screen or ice,
my untapped skills were plentiful, I'd get there in a trice.

But through the years my dreams were lost, the stars
    seemed far away,
My home, my job, my family dictated each new day.

Then suddenly a space appeared, demands became much
    less.
I found I'd time to stop and stare, to see beyond the mess.

The busyness of family life has now begun to ease.
Is now the time to dream again, to look beyond the trees?

No longer drawn to stage or screen, my dreams are more
    mundane,
a morning walk, some friends, some talk; to socialise
    again.

I recognise my skills don't lie in blades on skating rink,
but rather in a well cooked meal and friends' help at the
    sink.

I'll never do a bungy jump – it's those arthritic knees.
I'll never be a skating star, Jayne Torvill will be pleased.

But it won't stop me dreaming, there's still so much to do,
and Grannies can bring so much fun on visits to the zoo.

It's hard for us to picture when we are only three,
the joy that comes from people, and our friends as
    company.

Dorothy Tinsley
22 May 1996

Dot had not written poetry before. Why don't you have a go?

The next step

With the help of my God I shall leap over the wall.
Psalm 18.29

Perhaps 'the wall' for us is what constricts and limits us – our
fears and our prejudices – but we can 'leap over' to a new life.
Knowing where your strength lies will help you take the first
step into your new life. Valuing yourself will give you the
courage to tackle it. Being alert to the voice of God in prayer,
meditation, through the beauty of the earth, or the goodness
of women and men, will enable you to discover and follow his
will for you.

The next step might be to try doing something you have
never done before. For example, you could:

- learn a language
- go to a Keep Fit class
- climb a mountain
- swim down a river
- walk by the sea
- dance barefoot in the moonlight.

Here are some guidelines to follow in your new life:

- Mix with people who help you feel positive, excite and encourage you.
- Place yourself in stretching situations.
- Extend and broaden your network of friends and contacts to include those of different ages, backgrounds and faiths.
- Ask questions and seek advice.
- Plan ahead. Evaluate what you have done.
- Be open to receive feedback and criticism and use it.
- Seize the chance to have new experiences, take risks.
- Think things out for yourself instead of accepting others' views.
- Challenge your assumptions about your constraints.
- Choose to read, watch and listen to those things that you find true, beautiful and life-enhancing.
- Let go of old patterns, identify your values and clarify your goals.

Finally, beloved, whatever is true, whatever is honourable, whatever is just, whatever is pure, whatever is pleasing, whatever is commendable, if there is any excellence and if there is anything worthy of praise, think about these things. Keep on doing the things you have learned and received and heard and seen in me, and the peace of God will be with you.

Philippians 4.8–9

— *Appendix 1* —

Running confidence courses

With Rosemary Tucker, an experienced trainer, and alone, I have run a number of short introductory courses on confidence-building. Although these have been brief, a whole day or four evenings, there has been a sense of excitement, and group members have reported taking small but significant steps to improve their lives. Sometimes they have tried tackling a long-standing problem in a different way. One woman described how her mother disparaged everything she did and put her down. She was able to tell her mother how this made her feel for the first time.

All the material we used is contained in Chapters 3–6. It is based on the work of Linda Richardson, who is a freelance trainer, and I am grateful for her permission to reproduce it. If you have the training or experience, you could use it to run courses of your own or as a basis for discussion groups. I suggest that you do not try to cover all the material, but select the bits you feel happiest with.

Rosemary and I found that it was important to be relaxed, friendly and enthusiastic and affirm all contributions made by course members. We started by getting them to introduce themselves and say something positive about themselves, describing either 'a gift I bring to the Church', or 'something I have done recently that I am proud of'. It is important for the course leaders to 'model' this; they should say something about themselves that is true, but unlikely to make anyone feel inadequate. They should also be encouraging, affirmative and positive. This exercise will give a clearer idea of just how low members' level of confidence is.

If you decide to run a course, when you get to the part about events in childhood, I recommend caution. Unless it is a therapeutic group, run by someone trained in this work, it is not the place to handle deep trauma. We always offer to talk to people individually in the break or at the end of the session and advise seeking professional help if it seems necessary.

Here are some pointers you may find helpful in running a confidence-building course:

- Keep making the point that we are all different. Group members may not agree with what you say, and that is OK.
- Leave space for discussion after presenting each section.
- Give examples and amusing anecdotes.
- Make them laugh to relax any tension.
- Be aware of their reaction to what is said, the odd tear being wiped away.
- Let group members share in twos and threes and contribute to the larger session only as much as they want to.

— *Appendix 2* —

Voluntary work

You may have some spare time and feel you would like to offer your help, to a charity, your local hospital or parish church, for example.

- If lack of confidence is preventing you from volunteering, try pretending – behave as if you are perfectly confident.
- Decide how much time you can spare, halve it and offer that.
- Before you undertake any work, find out about any expenses involved. Who will pay? Can you afford travel expenses or materials you may be expected to pay for? (You are offering your time – not necessarily money – as a gift.)
- Don't let yourself be put upon.

When you apply, be clear in your own mind about what you want out of doing the work. State your reasons openly if asked. For example:

- 'I would like to feel more involved in the church.'
- 'I have always been interested in disabled people, because my brother is handicapped.'
- 'I would like a reason to get out of the house more.'
- 'Now that my husband has died, I need to feel useful.'
- 'I would like to meet new people.'

Recognizing and acknowledging our own need does not invalidate the help we offer others. It makes it more honest. Martyrs must be difficult friends!

You could contact one of the following (look them up in the telephone book or ask at your public library if necessary):

- your local Citizens Advice Bureau
- the Volunteer Bureau
- Age Concern
- WRVS
- The Red Cross
- your local hospital or hospice
- nursery, primary or secondary schools.

— Further Reading —

On assertiveness:

Dewar, F., *Living for a Change*. Darton, Longman & Todd 1988.
Dickson, A., *A Woman in Your Own Right*. Quartet 1982-94.
Harris, T. A., *I'm OK, You're OK*. Pan 1967.
Hopson, B. and Scally, M., *Build Your Own Rainbow*. Lifeskills Associates 1984.
Jeffers, S., *Feel the Fear and Do It Anyway*. Arrow 1991.
Sanford, L. T. and Donovan, M. E., *Women and Self-Esteem*. Penguin 1984.
Willis, L. and Daisley, J., *Springboard*. Hawthorn 1990.

On women and the Church:

Borrowdale, A., *Distorted Images*. SPCK 1991.
—, *A Woman's Work: Changing Christian Attitudes*. SPCK 1989.
Furlong, M., *A Dangerous Delight*. SPCK 1991.
—, *Feminine in the Church*. SPCK 1984.

Services and Prayers for women:

Furlong, M. and The St Hilda Community. *Women Included*. SPCK 1996.
Ward, H., Wild, J. and Morley, J., *Celebrating Women*. SPCK 1995.

On prayer and meditation:

Bloom, A., *School for Prayer*. Darton, Longman & Todd 1970.
Pilkington, E., *Learning to Pray*. Darton, Longman & Todd 1986.
Williams, H. A., *Becoming What I Am*. Darton, Longman & Todd 1980.

The Society for Promoting Christian Knowledge (SPCK) was founded in 1698. It has as its purpose three main tasks:

- **Communicating the Christian faith in its rich diversity**
- **Helping people to understand the Christian faith and to develop their personal faith**
- **Equipping Christians for mission and ministry**

SPCK Worldwide serves the Church through Christian literature and communication projects in over 100 countries. Special schemes also provide books for those training for ministry in many parts of the developing world. SPCK Worldwide's ministry involves Churches of many traditions. This worldwide service depends upon the generosity of others and all gifts are spent wholly on ministry programmes, without deductions.

SPCK Bookshops support the life of the Christian community by making available a full range of Christian literature and other resources, and by providing support to bookstalls and book agents throughout the UK. SPCK Bookshops' mail order department meets the needs of overseas customers and those unable to have access to local bookshops.

SPCK Publishing produces Christian books and resources, covering a wide range of inspirational, pastoral, practical and academic subjects. Authors are drawn from many different Christian traditions, and publications aim to meet the needs of a wide variety of readers in the UK and throughout the world.

The Society does not necessarily endorse the individual views contained in its publications, but hopes they stimulate readers to think about and further develop their Christian faith.

For further information about the Society, please write to:
SPCK, Holy Trinity Church, Marylebone Road,
London NW1 4DU, United Kingdom.
Telephone: 0171 387 5282